金原瑞人
MY FAVORITES

FRANZ KAFKA
THE METAMORPHOSIS

青灯社

THE METAMORPHOSIS by Franz Kafka, translated by Stanley Appelbaum

Copyright © 1996 by Dover Publications, Inc.

Permissions arranged with Dover Publications, Inc.

through The English Agency (Japan) Ltd.

まえがき

1. ドイツ語の作品を英訳で読む？

　翻訳を始めてもう25年くらいになるが、英語から日本語への翻訳はじつに難しい。それにくらべれば、英語からフランス語、ドイツ語からスペイン語、スペイン語から英語などの翻訳はじつに楽だ……というのは言い過ぎかもしれないが、それでも英語↔日本語の翻訳と比べるとはるかに楽なのはまちがいない。

　たとえば、同時通訳の方からこんなことをうかがったことがある。

　「英語から日本語への同時通訳は非常に疲れる。内容にもよるが、ふたり交替で通訳をしていてもしんどいことがあるくらいだ。それにひきかえ、ヨーロッパの言葉同士の通訳なんて、びっくりするくらい楽。こないだ英語をフランス語に同時通訳していたおばさんなんか、編み物しながらやってた」

　多少の誇張はあるにせよ、そのくらいの差はあると思う。

　文の構造や単語がどれくらい異なっているか、どれくらい似ているか、それを考えるだけで違いはわかってもらえると思う。ということは、通訳も翻訳もずいぶん無理をしているということだ。無理をしているということは、オリジナルからどうしても、はずれてしまう、ずれてしまう、離れてしまう、ということ。通訳も訳者も、なるべくそれを少なくするよう必死の努

力をする……のだが、なんのなんの、日本語とヨーロッパの言葉の壁は高くて厚い。

その点、ヨーロッパ言語同士の場合、その壁がないとはいわないが、比較的、低くて薄い。

ということは、訳者の力量などにもよるだろうが一般的にいって、ヨーロッパ言語の作品は日本語訳より英訳のほうがオリジナルに近い。

論より証拠で、『変身』の最初のページから一部分、ドイツ語の原文と、その英語訳を抜き出してみよう。

Gregors Blick richtete sich dann zum Fenster, und das trübe Wetter — man hörte Regentropfen auf das Fensterblech aufschlagen — machte ihn ganz melancholisch. »Wie wäre es, wenn ich noch ein wenig weiterschliefe und alle Narrheiten vergäße«, dachte er,

Gregor's gaze then turned toward the window, and the dismal weather — you could hear raindrops beating against the window gutter — made him quite melancholy. "What if I went back to sleep for another while and forgot all this foolishness?" he thought;

ほぼ1：1の対応ではないか。

なら、英語の好きな人や英語のできる人は、ヨーロッパ言語の作品を読みたければ日本語訳ではなく英訳で読めばいい。英語の勉強をしたい人にも勧めたい。これには次のようなメリットがある。

①日本語訳よりは原作に近いものを読める。
②日本語訳で読むより時間がかかるぶん、細かくじっくり読むことになり、理解が広がる。
③英語力がつく。

　そんなわけで、フランツ・カフカの『変身』の英訳本（Stanley Appelbaum 訳・DOVER PUBLICATIONS）に語注をつけてみた。ただし、高校や大学のリーダーのテキストとちがって、文法的な説明は最小限にとどめた。それは英文を読むのに文法が必要ないからではない。文法は言語の約束事をコンパクトにまとめた道具で、旅行をするときの地図のようなものだ。しっかりした地図を持っているかどうかは旅に大きく影響する。しかし、この本の目的は、英文と注をうまく使いながら、作品を読み、味わうことなので、文法的な説明は少なくしてある。

2．文法について

　語注では文法にはほとんど触れていないが、いくつか注意してほしいことがあるので、少しだけ書いておきたい。

　「使える英語」とかいう意味不明の言葉が流行し始めて以来、英語の授業から文法や読解の時間が減っていって、いまや会話中心になってきてしまった。しかし、小説やエッセイでは口語であまり使われない構文などがよく出てくる。

　たとえば分詞構文。これは用法が多岐にわたっているので、ここでは説明しないが、不安な方はぜひこれ

を機会に、文法や読解の参考書を読んで勉強してほしい。

それからもうひとつ、It is (was)...that の強調構文も会話ではあまり使われないので、苦手な人が多い。この『変身』の英訳にはよく出てくるので、簡単に説明しておこう。

たとえば "He met Gregor yesterday." という文のうち、'he' 'Gregor' 'yesterday' の3つをそれぞれ強調したい場合、次のように表現する。

・It was he that met Gregor yesterday.（昨日グレーゴルに会ったのは彼だ）
・It was Gregor that he met yesterday.（彼が昨日会ったのはグレーゴルだ）
・It was yesterday that he met Gregor.（彼がグレーゴルに会ったのは昨日だ）

It is (was)...that の強調構文を It が that 以下を受けていると勘違いすると意味がわからなくなるので注意してほしい。この強調構文、上の例のように単純な場合は気がつきやすいが、文が長くなったり複雑になったりすると、案外と難しい。この註釈本では何カ所か、指摘しておいた。

3．『変身』の舞台、その他について

さて、このカフカの『変身』だが、日本の読者にわかりづらいのが主人公グレーゴルの部屋の構造と、一家が住んでいる建物だろう。これについては、法政大学教授でカフカに詳しい新田誠吾さんに教えていただ

いた。新田さんのメールから引用させていただくとしよう。

ドイツ語では、戸建と集合住宅は別の単語です。『変身』の家は集合住宅です。翻訳でよく「控えの間」と訳されているのは、廊下にあたります。部屋の配置の手がかりは多くはありません。ロシア出身でアメリカの作家ウラジーミル・ナボコフも、部屋の配置について疑問に思い、考えたことがあります。グレーゴルの部屋には3つの扉があります。それぞれどこにつながっているのかを、物語を読みながらぜひ考えてみてください。

カフカは、『変身』の最初の部分を友だちに語って聴かせたことがあります。みんな笑ったそうです。そのときに同席した妹のオトラは「私の家の話じゃないの」と評したことが伝わっています。

それからもうひとつ、いったいこの物語の舞台はどこなのか、それもよくわからない。途中で 'a few gulden'、つまり「数グルデン」というお金の単位が出てくるが、グルデンは、ドイツ、オランダ、オーストリアその他の国々で使われている。その他の手がかりは「シャルロッテ通り」なのだが、これについては新田さんから次のようなメールをいただいた。

舞台については、物語上はどことも明示がありませんが、シャルロッテ通りとあるので、ドイツ語圏のど

こかだろうと推定されます。私の手元の資料では、当時のプラハ中心街にシャルロッテ通りは見当たりません。

　当時カフカは、ベルリンに住むユダヤ系女性フェリーセ・バウアーと知り合い、日に何通も手紙を出す関係でした。ベルリンには、フリードリヒ一世の妃シャルロッテにちなむ宮殿や通りがあったので、ひょっとすると恋人の痕跡を残そうとしたのかもしれません。

　つまり、不明ということ。
　さて、前置きはこれくらいにして、どうぞ、英語で読む『変身』の世界へ。

　　　　　　　　　　　　　　　　　　　金原瑞人

contents

まえがき　金原瑞人 ……… 3

The Metamorphosis ……… 11

あとがき　金原瑞人 ……… 167

装幀　眞島和馬

The Metamorphosis

I

When Gregor Samsa awoke from troubled dreams one morning, he found that he had been transformed in his bed into an enormous bug. He lay on his back, which was hard as armor, and, when he lifted his head a little, he saw his belly — rounded, brown, partitioned by archlike ridges — on top of which the blanket, ready to slip off altogether, was just barely perched. His numerous legs, pitifully thin in comparison to the rest of his girth, flickered helplessly before his eyes.

"What's happened to me?" he thought. It was no dream. His room, a real room meant for human habitation, though a little too small, lay peacefully within its four familiar walls. Above the table, on which an unpacked sampling of fabric swatches was strewn — Samsa was a traveling salesman — hung the picture that he had recently cut out of an illustrated magazine and had placed in a pretty gilt frame. It depicted a lady who, decked out in a fur hat and a fur boa, sat upright, raising toward the viewer a heavy fur muff in which her whole forearm was encased.

Gregor's gaze then turned toward the window, and the dismal weather — you could hear raindrops beating against the window gutter — made him quite melancholy. "What if I went back to sleep for another while and forgot all this foolishness?" he thought; but that was totally out of the question, because he was used to sleeping on his right side, and in his present state he

I

3 **Gregor Samsa** 独語読みだと「グレーゴル・ザムザ」、英語読みだと「グレガー・ザムザ」 **troubled dreams** いやな夢 5 **bug** 虫、昆虫。この作品で、ザムザがいったいどんな「虫」に変身したのかはよくわからない。ただ、あとに出てくるように「脚がたくさんある」虫らしい **lay on his back** あお向けに寝ていた 6 **which was hard as armor** which の先行詞は back (背中)。つまり、背中が鎧のように硬かった 7 **belly** 腹 **rounded** 丸い **partitioned** 区切られている 8 **archlike ridges** アーチのようになった起伏 9 **barely perched** ずり落ちかけている **numerous** とてもたくさんの 10 **In comparison to the rest of his girth** 彼の胴体のほかの部分とくらべて 11 **flickered helplessly** 情けなく揺れていた

13 **meant for human habitation** 人が住むべきところとして作られた 14 **lay peacefully** (部屋は) 平和に存在している (いつものようにそこにある) 16 **fabric swatches** 織物の見本 **was strewn** 散らばっていた 17 **traveling salesman** あちこち旅して商品を売るセールスマン 19 **pretty gilt frame** きれいな金縁の額 **depicted** 描いていた 20 **decked out** 着飾った **fur boa** 毛皮の襟巻き **raising toward the viewer a heavy fur muff** 見る人 (こちら) にむかって、ごつい毛皮のマフ (毛皮を筒状にした女性用の装身具で、手を入れて温めるもの) を差し出している 21 **her whole forearm was encased** 彼女の前腕が全部入っている

24 **dismal** うっとうしい 25 **window gutter** 窓の下についている樋 26 **sleep for another while** また、もう少し寝る 28 **out of the question** 問題外 29 **on his right side** 右下に **in his present state** 彼の今の状態 (状況) では

couldn't get into that position. No matter how energetically he threw himself onto his right side, each time he rocked back into the supine position. He must have tried a hundred times, closing his eyes to avoid seeing his squirming legs, not stopping until he began to feel a slight, dull pain in his side that he had never felt before.

"My God," he thought, "what a strenuous profession I've chosen! Traveling day in and day out. The turmoil of business is much greater than in the home office, and on top of that I'm subjected to this torment of traveling, to the worries about train connections, the bad meals at irregular hours, an intercourse with people that constantly changes, never lasts, never becomes cordial. The devil take it all!" He felt a slight itch up on his belly; slowly shoved himself on his back closer to the bedpost, so he could lift his head better; found the itchy place, which was all covered with little white spots that he was unable to diagnose; and wanted to feel the area with one leg, but drew it back immediately, because when he touched it he was invaded by chills.

He slid back into his former position. "Getting up early like this," he thought, "makes you totally idiotic. People must have their sleep. Other traveling salesmen live like harem women. For instance, when during the course of the morning I go back to the hotel to copy out the orders I've received, those fine gentlemen are just having their breakfast. I should try that with my boss; I'd be fired on the spot. Anyway, who knows whether that wouldn't be a good thing for me after all. If I didn't

1 **energetically** 必死になって   3 **rocked back into the supine position** ごろんと、あお向けにもどってしまう   5 **squirming legs** もぞもぞ動く脚   **not stopping until...** 〜になるまでやめなかった。〜になって、やっとやめた

7 **My God** まったく   **strenuous** しんどい   8 **day in and day out** 毎日毎日   **turmoil** 大変さ   9 **home office** 会社   10 **on top of that** そのうえ   **I'm subjected to...** 〜を引き受けなくてはならない   **torment** 苦しみ、いやなこと   11 **worries** 心配   **train connections** 列車の乗り継ぎ   12 **intercourse** 付き合い   13 **never lasts** 決して長続きしない   **cordial** 打ち解ける   **The devil (should) take it all!** 悪魔がそれを持っていってくれますように！　悪魔にでもくれてやる！   14 **itch** かゆみ   15 **shoved** 体を動かす   **bedpost** ベッドの四隅の柱   18 **diagnose** 診断できる、どんな病気かわかる   **feel the area with one leg** 1本の脚でその部分にさわる   19 **immediately** すぐに   20 **chills** 寒気、ぞっとすること

21 **Getting up early like this...makes you totally idiotic.** Getting up early like this が主語で、動詞が makes。こんなふうに早く起きると、頭が完全にいかれてしまう   22 **idiotic** ばか   24 **harem** ハレム、イスラム教国の王室の後宮、女性が大切に扱われる   **during the course of the morning** 午前中に   25 **copy out the orders** 注文をすべて写す   27 **I should try that with my boss** うちの社長にそれをやろうものなら   28 **I'd be fired** くびになるだろう   **on the spot** その場で   **Anyway** とにかく、だけど   **who knows whether that wouldn't be a good thing** それが悪いことかどうかなんてだれにもわからない   29 **after all** 結局、しょせん

hold myself back because of my parents, I would have quit long ago; I would have walked right up to the boss and let my heart out to him. He would surely have fallen off his desk! That's a peculiar habit of his, too, sitting on his desk and talking down to his employees from up above; and, besides, they have to step way up close because the boss is so hard of hearing. Now, I haven't given up all hope yet; once I have the money together to pay off my parents' debt to him — that should still take five or six years — I'll definitely go through with it. Then I'll make the big break. At the moment, of course, I've got to get up, because my train leaves at five."

And he glanced over toward his alarm clock, which was ticking on the wardrobe. "Father in Heaven!" he thought. It was half past six, and the hands were moving ahead peacefully; in fact, it was later than half past, it was almost a quarter to seven. Could the alarm have failed to ring? From the bed he could see that it was correctly set for four; surely, it had also rung. Yes, but was it possible to sleep peacefully through that furniture-shaking ring? Well, he hadn't slept peacefully, but probably all the more soundly for that. Yet, what should he do now? The next train left at seven; to catch it he would have had to make a mad dash, his sample case wasn't packed yet, and he himself definitely didn't feel particularly fresh and lively. And even if he caught the train, he couldn't escape a bawling out from his boss, because the office messenger had waited at the five-o'clock train and had long since made a report about his

1 **hold myself back** 自制する 2 **quit**（仕事を）やめる 3 **let my heart out** 思っていることを吐き出す 4 **That's** この That は sitting ～ up above **peculiar habit of his** 社長の変わった癖 5 **talking down to ～** ～に対して見下した調子で話す **employees** 従業員、使用人たち 6 **besides** そのうえ **step way up close**（way は強調）ぐっと近寄る 7 **hard of hearing** 耳が遠い 8 **once**（接続詞）いったん～になったら 9 **take five or six years** 5、6年かかる 10 **definitely** 絶対に **go through with it** それをやりとげる 11 **big break** でっかいチャンス **At the moment** 今は

14 **wardrobe** ワードローブ（洋服だんす） **Father in Heaven**（Oh, my God と同じ）なんてことだ 15 **the hands** 時計の針 17 **have failed to ring** 鳴らなかった 18 **was correctly set for four** ちゃんと4時に合わせてある 19 **surely, it had also rung** まちがいなく、鳴ったのだ 20 **furniture-shaking ring** 家具が揺れるほどの音 22 **all the more** よけいに **soundly** ぐっすり **for that** そのせいで（he hadn't slept peacefully） **Yet** しかし 23 **to catch it** その列車に乗るためには 24 **a mad dash** 必死に走ること 26 **particularly** とくに **fresh and lively** 元気はつらつ 27 **escape a bawling out from his boss** 社長から怒鳴られるのを避ける 29 **long since** ずっと前に

negligence. He was a creature of the boss's, spineless and stupid. Now, what if he reported in sick? But that would be extremely distressing and suspicious, because during his five years' employment Gregor had not been ill even once. The boss would surely arrive with the health-insurance doctor, would complain to his parents about their lazy son and would cut short all objections by referring them to the health-insurance doctor, in whose eyes the only people that exist at all are perfectly healthy specimens who are work-shy. And besides, would he be so wrong in this case? Actually, aside from a truly excessive drowsiness after all that sleep, Gregor felt quite well and in fact was particularly hungry.

While he was considering all this in the greatest haste, still unable to decide whether to get out of bed — the clock was just striking six forty-five — there was a cautious knock on the door at the head of his bed. "Gregor," a voice called — it was his mother — "it's six forty-five. Didn't you intend to make a trip?" That gentle voice! Gregor was frightened when he heard his own answering voice, which, to be sure, was unmistakably his accustomed one, but in which there now appeared, as if rising from below, an irrepressible, painful peeping sound, so that his words retained their clarity only at the very outset but became distorted as they faded away, so that you couldn't tell if you had heard them correctly. Gregor had meant to give a detailed answer and explain everything, but under the circumstances he merely said: "Yes, yes; thanks, Mother; I'm getting up now."

1 negligence 怠慢 a creature of the boss's 社長の奴隷 spineless 背骨がない、根性がない 2 reported in sick 病欠だと報告する 3 extremely とても distressing 悲惨な、よくない suspicious 疑いを起こさせる 5 arrive with the health-insurance doctor 保険医を連れてやってくる 7 cut short 無視する objections 反論、言い訳 8 referring them to the health-insurance doctor 保険医に（言い訳を）まかせる、まわす 10 specimens 人間 work-shy 仕事嫌い、なまけ者 11 he 保険医 12 excessive drowsiness 猛烈な眠さ 13 felt quite well とても気分がよく感じた particularly 非常に 14 in the greatest haste 大急ぎで 16 cautious knock ひかえめなノック 19 intend to make a trip セールスに出るつもり 20 was frightened ぎょっとした 21 was unmistakably his accustomed one まちがいなく、いつもの自分の声 (one は voice のこと) 22 there now appeared そのとき、現れた 23 an irrepressible, painful peeping sound 押さえきれない、痛々しい、ピーという音 24 retained their clarity 明確さを保持していた 25 outset 最初 distorted as they faded away ゆがんで、消えてしまった 26 tell わかる 27 had meant to するつもりだった a detailed answer 詳しい答え 28 under the circumstances 今の状況では

Because the door was made of wood, the alteration in Gregor's voice was probably not noticeable, since his mother was pacified by that explanation and shuffled away. But as a result of that brief conversation the other members of the family had become aware that, contrary to expectation, Gregor was still at home; and his father was soon knocking at one of the side doors, softly, but with his fist. "Gregor, Gregor," he called, "what's going on?" And before very long he admonished him again, in a deeper voice: "Gregor! Gregor!" But at the other side door his sister was quietly lamenting: "Gregor? Aren't you well? Do you need anything?" Gregor answered in both directions: "Be right there!" He made an effort, by enunciating most carefully and by inserting long pauses between the individual words, to free his voice of anything out of the ordinary. His father then returned to his breakfast, but his sister whispered: "Gregor, open up, I beg you." But Gregor had not the slightest intention of opening the door; in fact, he was now glad he had formed the cautious habit, an offshoot of his business trips, of locking all his doors at night even at home.

First he wanted to get up in peace and unmolested, get dressed and, especially, have breakfast, and only afterwards give the matter further thought, because, as he now realized, in bed he would never arrive at any sensible conclusion to his musings. He recalled that, often in the past, while in bed, he had felt some slight pain or other, perhaps caused by lying in an awkward position, and that, when he got out of bed, the pain had proved to

1 **alteration** 変化　3 **was pacified** 安心した　**shuffled away** 足を引きずるようにして離れていった　4 **the other members of the family** ほかの家族　5 **had become aware that** すでに気がついていた（気がついていた内容は Gregor was still at home）　**contrary to expectation** 予想に反して　7 **side doors** 横からの入口（グレーゴルの部屋にはいくつかドアがある）　**softly, but with his fist** 軽く、しかし、こぶしで　8 **what's going on?** いったいどうしたんだ？　9 **admonished** 注意をうながす　11 **his sister** グレーゴルの妹なのか姉なのかここではまだ不明（そのうち「妹」だということがわかる）　**was quietly lamenting** 小声で不安そうにいった　12 **in both directions** 両方向に（父親と妹に）　13 **Be right there!** そこにいてくれ！　かまわないでくれ！　14 **enunciating** はっきり発音すること　15 **between the individual words** 一語一語の間に　**to free his voice of anything out of the ordinary**（free ① of ② で「①から②を除く、取る」）彼の声から普通でないものを取りのぞくために、声が普通に聞こえるように　17 **open up** ドアを開けて　18 **I beg you** お願いだから　**had not the slightest intention of opening the door** ドアを開けるつもりはまったくなかった　20 **cautious habit** 注意深くする習慣　**an offshoot** 産物

22 **unmolested** 邪魔のない状態　24 **give the matter further thought** このことをさらに考える　25 **would never arrive at any sensible conclusion** なんら現実的な結論に至ることはないだろう　26 **musings** 考え　**recalled** 思い出した　**often in the past** 過去にたびたび　27 **some slight pain or other** 軽い痛みのようなもの　28 **awkward position** 変な姿勢　29 **had proved to be purely imaginary** ただの想像にすぎなかったことがわかった

be purely imaginary; and he was eager to find out how his impressions of that morning would gradually be dispelled. That the alteration in his voice was nothing more than the harbinger of a nasty cold, a professional hazard of traveling salesmen, he had not the slightest doubt.

To throw off the blanket was quite easy; all he needed to do was puff himself up a little and it fell down by itself. But after that things became difficult, especially since he was so unusually wide. He would normally have used his arms and hands to hoist himself up; but instead of them he now had only the numerous little legs, which were uninterruptedly moving in the most confused way and which, in addition, he couldn't control. Whenever he intended to bend one of them, at first he extended it; and when he finally succeeded in executing his wishes with that particular leg, all of the others meanwhile would thrash about as if they were completely independent, in an extreme, painful agitation. "But I can't stay in bed doing nothing," Gregor said to himself.

First he wanted to leave the bed with the lower part of his body, but this lower part, which, by the way, he hadn't seen yet and of which he couldn't form any clear idea, either, proved to be too difficult to move around; the procedure was so slow; and when finally, having grown almost wild, he gathered all his strength and pushed forward heedlessly, he went in the wrong direction and collided violently with the lower bedpost. The burning pain that he felt taught him that it was precisely

The Metamorphosis

2 **impressions** 感じたこと **be dispelled** なくなる 4 **harbinger** 前兆 **nasty cold** ひどい風邪 **professional hazard of traveling salesmen** セールスマンという職業につきものの危険、職業上かかりやすい病気 5 **had not the slightest doubt** まったく疑っていなかった

6 **throw off** はねのける 7 **puff himself up** 自分をふくらませる、体をふくらませる 9 **since**（接続詞）なぜなら 10 **hoist himself up** 体を起こす 11 **instead of them** それら（腕や手）のかわりに 12 **uninterruptedly** せわしく **in the most confused way** めちゃくちゃに 13 **in addition** おまけに 15 **executing his wishes with that particular leg** その脚を思うように動かすこと 17 **thrash about** 勝手に動く 18 **painful agitation** 嘆かわしいほどの（どうしようもない）興奮状態

22 **by the way** ところで 23 **of which** それ（下半身）については **couldn't form any clear idea** はっきりしたイメージがつかめない 24 **proved to be too difficult to move around**（主語は this lower part）動きまわることがとてもむつかしいことがわかった 25 **procedure** 進行、動き **having grown almost wild** かっとなって 26 **gathered all his strength** 全身の力をこめた 27 **heedlessly** 不注意に、力まかせに 28 **collided** ぶつかった **The burning pain that he felt** 彼の感じた激しい痛み 29 **precisely** まちがいなく

the lower part of his body that was perhaps the most sensitive at the moment.

Therefore, he tried to get the upper part of his body out of bed first, and carefully turned his head toward the edge of the bed. He managed to do this easily and, despite its width and weight, finally the bulk of his body slowly followed in the direction his head had turned. But when at last he had moved his head into the open space outside the bed, he became afraid of continuing to edge forward in this manner, because if he finally let himself fall like that, it would take a real miracle to keep his head from being injured. And now of all times he must take every precaution not to lose consciousness; rather than that, he would stay in bed.

But when once again, heaving a sigh after similar efforts, he lay there just as before, and once again saw his little legs battling one another even more pitifully, if that were possible — when he could find no possibility of bringing calm and order into that arbitrary turmoil — he told himself again that he couldn't possibly stay in bed, and that the most sensible thing was to make every sacrifice if there existed even the smallest hope of thereby freeing himself from bed. But at the same time he didn't forget to remind himself occasionally that the calmest possible reflection is far preferable to desperate decisions. At such moments he would direct his eyes as fixedly as possible toward the window, but unfortunately there was not much confidence or cheer to be derived from the sight of the morning fog, which even shrouded

The Metamorphosis

2 **at the moment** いまのところは

3 **Therefore** そこで 5 **the edge of the bed** ベッドの端 **managed** できた 6 **despite its width and weight** その幅と重さにもかかわらず（its はそのあとの the bulk of his body） **the bulk of his body** 体の本体（胴体） 8 **open space outside the bed** ベッドの外の空間 9 **continuing** 続ける 10 **edge forward** 少しずつ突きだす **in this manner** こんなふうにして（同じようにして） 11 **it would take a real miracle to keep his head from being injured** 頭にひどい怪我をするのを避けるには本物の奇跡を必要とするだろう、よっぽどの奇跡でも起こらないかぎり、絶対、頭にひどい怪我をするだろう 12 **now of all times** とくにいまは 13 **precaution** 注意 14 **rather than that** それよりはむしろ

15 **heaving a sigh** ため息をついて 17 **battling one another** 相争う **more pitifully** それまで以上にあさましい、情けない **if that were possible** もしそんなことが可能なら 19 **bringing calm and order** 冷静さと秩序をもたらす **arbitrary turmoil** 無節操な混乱状態（脚の様子） 21 **sensible** 理性的な **make every sacrifice** あらゆる犠牲をはらう、必死に努力する 22 **if there existed even the smallest hope** もし、かすかでも希望があるのなら 23 **thereby** それ（犠牲）によって **freeing himself from bed** ベッドから自由になる 24 **occasionally** ときどき **the calmest** とても冷静な 25 **possible reflection** 現実的なことを考えること **preferable to desperate decisions** やけっぱちの（自暴自棄の）決心より望ましい 26 **as fixedly as possible** できるだけしっかりと 28 **confidence or cheer** 確信も元気も **be derived from the sight of the morning fog** 朝霧をみることから引き出される 29 **shrouded** おおっていた

the other side of the narrow street. "Seven o'clock already," he said to himself as the clock struck again, "seven o'clock already and still such a fog." And for a little while he lay there calmly, breathing very gently, as if perhaps expecting the total silence to restore him to his real, understandable condition.

But then he said to himself: "Before it strikes seven fifteen, I just have to be all the way out of bed. Besides, by that time someone from the firm will come to ask about me, because the office opens before seven o'clock." And now he prepared to rock his entire body out of bed at its full length in a uniform movement. If he let himself fall out of bed in this manner, he expected that his head, which he intended to lift up high during the fall, would receive no injury. His back seemed to be hard; when falling onto the carpet, surely nothing would happen to it. His greatest fear was the thought of the loud crash which must certainly result, and which would probably cause, if not a scare, then at least concern on the other side of all the doors. But that risk had to be taken.

When Gregor was already projecting halfway out of bed — this new method was more of a game than a hard task, all he needed to do was keep on rocking back and forth in short spurts — it occurred to him how simple everything would be if someone came to help him. Two strong people — he thought of his father and the maid — would have completely sufficed; they would only have had to shove their arms under his rounded back,

₃ **still such a fog** まだこんな霧が ₅ **the total silence** まったくの沈黙 **restore** 取りもどす ₆ **real, understandable condition** 現実的な、理解可能な状況

₈ **all the way** すっかり ₉ **the firm** 会社 ₁₁ **rock his entire body out of bed** 全身を揺らしてベッドから出す ₁₂ **at its full length** 手足をのばした状態で **in a uniform movement** 体の動きをそろえて ₁₃ **in this manner** そんなふうに ₁₅ **His back seemed to be hard** 背中はかたそうだ ₁₇ **the loud crash**（落ちたときの）大きな音 ₁₈ **which must certainly result** 絶対起こるにきまっている ₁₉ **cause** 引き起こす **if not a scare** ぎょっとさせることはないとしても **concern** 心配 **on the other side of all the doors** すべてのドアの向こう側で

₂₂ **projecting** 突きだしている ₂₃ **more of a game than a hard task** つらい仕事というより楽しいゲーム ₂₄ **rocking back and forth** 体を揺らすこと ₂₅ **in short spurts** 短い間隔で激しく ₂₈ **sufficed** 十分である ₂₉ **shove** 突っこむ、差しこむ **rounded back** 丸い背中

extract him from bed that way like a nut from its shell, stoop down under his bulk and then merely wait cautiously until he had swung himself entirely over on the floor, where hopefully his little legs would find their use. Now, completely apart from the fact that the doors were locked, should he really have called for help? Despite all his tribulations, he was unable to suppress a smile at that thought.

He had now proceeded so far that, when rocking more vigorously, he could barely still maintain his equilibrium, and would very soon have to reach a definitive decision, because in five minutes it would be seven fifteen — when there was a ring at the apartment door. "That's somebody from the firm," he said to himself and nearly became rigid, while his little legs danced all the more quickly. For a moment everything remained quiet. "They aren't opening," Gregor said to himself, enmeshed in some unreasoning hope. But then, naturally, just as always, the maid went to the door with a firm tread and opened it. Gregor needed only to hear the visitor's first words of greeting and he already knew who it was — the chief clerk himself. Why was only Gregor condemned to work for a firm where people immediately conceived the greatest suspicions at the smallest sign of negligence? Were all employees simply scoundrels, was there among them not one loyal, devoted person who, even though he had merely failed to utilize a couple of morning hours on behalf of the firm, had become crazed by pangs of conscience, to the

1 **extract** 引っぱる　**a nut from its shell** 木の実を殻から（引っぱり出すように）　2 **stoop down** 体をかがめる　**his bulk** 彼の胴体　3 **until he had swung himself entirely over on the floor** 床の上で寝返りを打つまで　4 **hopefully his little legs would find their use** うまくいけば、たくさんの小さな脚が役立ってくれるだろう　5 **apart from the fact that** that 以下のこととは別にして　7 **Despite all his tribulations** 苦しい状況にもかかわらず　**suppress a smile** 笑いをおさえる　8 **at that thought** そんなことを考えると

9 **proceeded so far that** that 以下のところまできていた　10 **vigorously** 激しく　**maintain his oquilibrium** バランスを保つ　11 **a definitive decision** 最終決定　12 **in five minutes** 5分後には　15 **rigid** 体がこわばる　**all the more** それまで以上に　17 **They aren't opening** 家の者は玄関のドアを開けない、だれも出ない　18 **enmeshed** とらわれた　**unreasoning hope** ばかげた希望　20 **firm tread** しっかりした足取り　22 **chief clerk** 事務長　23 **condemned** 運命づけられている　24 **conceived the greatest suspicions** 大きな疑いをかける　**at the smallest sign of negligence** ほんのささいな怠慢らしきもの　26 **scoundrels** ろくでなし、ひどい人間　27 **devoted** 献身的な　28 **utilize** 使う　**on behalf of the firm** 会社のために　29 **crazed** 発狂する　**pangs of conscience** 良心の呵責　**to the point of ～** ～にまでいたっている

point of being incapable of getting out of bed? Wouldn't it really have been enough to send an apprentice to ask — if all this questioning was necessary at all — did the chief clerk himself have to come, thereby indicating to the entire innocent family that the investigation into this suspicious incident could only be entrusted to the intelligence of the chief clerk? And, more as a result of the irritation that these reflections caused Gregor, than as a result of a proper decision, he swung himself out of bed with all his might. There was a loud thump, but it wasn't a real crash. The fall was deadened somewhat by the carpet, and in addition Gregor's back was more resilient than he had thought, so that the muffled sound wasn't so noticeable. But he hadn't held his head carefully enough and had bumped it; he turned it and rubbed it against the carpet in vexation and pain.

"Something fell in there," said the chief clerk in the room on the left side. Gregor tried to imagine whether the chief clerk might not some day have an experience similar to his of today: the possibility really had to be conceded. But, as if in brutal response to this question, the chief clerk now took a few determined steps in the adjoining room, which made his patent-leather boots squeak. From the room on the right side Gregor's sister whispered, to inform him: "Gregor, the chief clerk is here." "I know," said Gregor to himself, but he didn't dare to raise his voice so loud that his sister could hear him.

"Gregor," his father now said from the room on the

2 **apprentice** 見習い 3 **if all this questioning was necessary at all** こんなことを確かめにくるなんてことが必要だとしての話だが 4 **thereby** それによって、その結果 **indicating** 示す 5 **the entire innocent family** なんの責任もない家族みんな 6 **entrusted** まかせられている **intelligence** 裁断、判断 7 **more as a result of the irritation...than as a result of a proper decision** 適切な決心の結果としてではなくこの怒りの結果として 10 **with all his might** 全力で **thump**（床に）落ちる音 11 **a real crash** 激しい音 **deadened** 和らげられた 12 **resilient than he had thought** 思ったより柔らかかった、弾力があった 13 **muffled sound** 鈍い音 14 **noticeable** 目立つ 15 **had bumped it** 頭をぶつけた **turned it** 頭（首）を回した 16 **vexation** いらだち、腹立ち

17 **in there** そちらの（中の）ほうで 19 **experience similar to his of today** 今日の彼のと似た経験 22 **few determined steps** きっぱりとした数歩 **the adjoining room** 隣の部屋 23 **patent-leather** エナメル革 24 **squeak** きしむ 25 **inform** 知らせる 26 **he didn't dare to raise his voice** 思い切って声をあげることができなかった

left side, "the chief clerk has come and is inquiring why you didn't leave by the early train. We don't know what to tell him. Besides, he wants to talk with you personally. So please open the door. He will surely be kind enough to forgive the disorder in your room." "Good morning, Mr. Samsa," the chief clerk meanwhile called, in a friendly tone. "He isn't well," Gregor's mother said to the chief clerk while his father was still talking at the door, "he isn't well, believe me, sir. How otherwise would Gregor miss a train! The boy has no head for anything but the business. I'm almost upset, as it is, that he never goes out at night; he's been in town for eight days this time, but has stayed at home every night. He sits with us at the table and reads the paper quietly or studies timetables. It's already a distraction for him when he busies himself with fretsaw work. So, for example, during two or three evenings he carved a small frame; you'll be amazed how pretty it is; it's hanging in his room; you'll see it right away when Gregor opens up. Besides, I'm glad you're here, sir; on our own we couldn't have persuaded Gregor to open the door; he's so obstinate; and I'm sure he's not feeling well, even though he denied it earlier this morning." "I'll be right there," said Gregor slowly and deliberately, but not making a move, so as to lose not a word of the conversation. "I, too, my dear lady, can think of no other explanation," said the chief clerk; "I hope it's nothing serious. Although I am also bound to state that we business people — unfortunately or fortunately, according

The Metamorphosis

1 **is inquiring** たずねている 2 **don't know what to tell him** 彼になんといっていいかわからない 3 **personally** ふたりきりで 5 **disorder** 散らかっていること 9 **believe me** 本当なんです **otherwise** そうでなければ 10 **The boy has no head for** あの子は興味がない 11 **anything but the business** 仕事以外は何にも **upset** 困ってしまう **as it is** 実際のところ 15 **studies timetables** 時刻表を調べる **distraction** 趣味、娯楽 16 **busies himself with** 〜で忙しい **fretsaw work** 糸鋸を使って物を作ること **for example** たとえば 17 **carved a small frame** 小さな額を作った 19 **right away** すぐに **opens up** 部屋のドアを開ける 20 **on our own** わたしたちだけでは 22 **obstinate** 頑固な、聞きわけがない 23 **I'll be right there** すぐそこにいく 24 **deliberately** ゆっくり **not making a move** 動かないで 25 **so as to lose not a word of the conversation** 会話をひとこともきもらさないように 28 **bound to state** いわなくてはならない 29 **unfortunately or fortunately** 幸か不幸か **according to how you look at it** 考え方によりますが

to how you look at it — very often simply have to overcome a slight indisposition out of regard for the business." "Well, can the gentleman go in to see you now?" asked the impatient father, and knocked on the door again. "No," said Gregor. In the room on the left side a painful silence ensued, in the room on the right side the sister began to sob.

Why didn't the sister go and join the others? She had probably just gotten out of bed and hadn't even begun dressing. And why was she crying? Because he didn't get up and let the chief clerk in? Because he was in danger of losing his job, and because then his boss would once more dun their parents for his old claims? For the time being those were needless worries, after all. Gregor was still here and hadn't the slightest thought of abandoning his family. At the moment he was lying there on the carpet, and no one acquainted with his current state could seriously have asked him to let in the chief clerk. But, after all, Gregor couldn't really be discharged at once on account of this slight discourtesy, for which a suitable excuse would easily be found later on. And it seemed to Gregor that it would be much more sensible to leave him in peace for now instead of disturbing him with tears and exhortations. But it was precisely all the uncertainty that was oppressing the others and that excused their behavior.

"Mr. Samsa," the chief clerk now called in a louder voice, "what's going on? You're barricading yourself in your room, giving just 'yes' and 'no' answers, causing

1 **simply** まったく、本当に（強調）　2 **a slight indisposition** 軽い病気、軽い体調不良　**out of regard for the business** 仕事のためであれば　3 **the gentleman** 事務長のこと　4 **impatient** いらいらしている　5 **a painful silence** いたたまれない沈黙　6 **ensued** 生まれた

8 **join the others** ほかの家族に加わる　12 **then** そうなった場合、そうすると　13 **dun** 催促する　**old claims** 昔の借金　**For the time being** さしあたりは、当分は　14 **needless worries** 不要な心配　15 **hadn't the slightest thought** 少しも考えていない　**abandoning his family** 家族を捨てる　16 **At the moment** 今のところは　17 **acquainted with** 知っている　18 **let in** 入れる　19 **be discharged** くびになる　20 **discourtesy** 無礼、不作法　**for which** それ（this slight discourtesy）に対しては　21 **suitable excuse** それにふさわしい（適当な）言い訳　**later on** あとで　22 **sensible** 賢明な　23 **leave him in peace** 事務長を刺激しないでおく　**instead of disturbing him with tears and exhortations** 事務長を涙や説得で不快にさせないで　24 **But it was...that...their behavior.** (it was...that の強調構文で、all the uncertainty が主語) まさにこのはっきりしない状況こそが、家族を不安にさせ、こういう行動（態度）を取らせていたのだ　28 **barricading** 閉じこめる　29 **giving just 'yes' and 'no' answers** 「はい」とか「いいえ」とかいうだけで

your parents big, needless worries and — to mention this just incidentally — neglecting your business duties in a truly unheard-of fashion. I am speaking here in the name of your parents and of your employer, and I am asking you quite seriously for an immediate, lucid explanation. I'm amazed, I'm amazed. I thought I knew you for a calm, sensible person, and now suddenly you apparently want to begin making an exhibition of peculiar caprices. To be sure, early this morning our employer, when speaking to me, hinted at a possible explanation for your negligence — it concerned the cash receipts that were recently entrusted to you — but, honestly, I all but gave him my word of honor that that explanation couldn't be the true one. Now, however, I see your incomprehensible stubbornness here and I am losing all willingness to say a good word for you in the slightest way. Nor is your position by any means the most solid. I originally had the intention of telling you all this between ourselves, but since you are making me waste my time here pointlessly, I don't know why your parents shouldn't hear it, too. Well, then, your performance recently has been most unsatisfactory; true, this isn't the season for doing especially good business, we acknowledge that; but a season for doing no business at all just doesn't exist, Mr. Samsa, it can't be allowed to exist." "But, sir," Gregor called out in distraction, forgetting everything else in his excitement, "I'm going to open the door immediately, this minute. A slight indisposition, a dizzy spell, have prevented me from

1 **to mention this** これをいわせてもらうが 2 **just incidentally** ついでに 3 **unheard-of fashion** いままできいたこともないけしからん方法で **in the name of** 〜の名において、〜の代わりに 4 **employer** 社長 5 **lucid** 明快な 8 **apparently** みたところ、どうやら **making an exhibition** 披露する 9 **peculiar caprices** 妙な気まぐれ 10 **hinted at** ほのめかした **possible explanation** 考えられる説明 11 **concerned** 関係していた 12 **cash receipts** 現金の受け取り **entrusted to you** きみにまかせた 13 **all but** (= almost) **my word of honor** 自分の名誉にかけての言葉 15 **Incomprehensible stubbornness** 理解できない頑固さ 16 **willingness** やる気 **say a good word for you** きみを弁護する言葉 **in the slightest way** どんなにささいな方法であっても 17 **by any means** まったく 18 **solid** 安定している **originally** もともとは、最初は 19 **between ourselves** ふたりきりで **since** (接続詞) 〜だから 20 **pointlessly** 無意味に **I don't know why your parents shouldn't hear it** きみの両親にきこえてもかまわない 21 **performance** 成績、成果 24 **acknowledge** 認める **a season for doing no business at all just doesn't exist** まったく商売にならない時期なんてものは存在しない 25 **it can't be allowed to exist** あってはならない 26 **in distraction** 思わず 29 **a dizzy spell** めまいの発作

getting up. I'm still lying in bed. But now I feel quite lively again. I am just now climbing out of bed. Be patient for just another moment! I'm not quite as well yet as I thought. But I now feel all right. The things that can affect a person! Just last evening I felt perfectly fine, my parents know that; or it might be better to say that even last evening I had a little advance indication. People should have noticed it from the way I looked. Why didn't I report it at the office?! But you always think that you'll be able to fight off an illness without having to stay home. Sir! Spare my parents! There is no basis for all the complaints you're now making against me; and no one has said a word to me about them. Perhaps you haven't read the last orders I sent in. Besides, I'll still make the trip on the eight-o'clock train, the couple of hours of rest have strengthened me. Don't waste your time here, sir; I'll be at the office myself in no time, and please be good enough to tell them that and give my best wishes to our employer!"

And while Gregor was pouring all of this out hastily, scarcely knowing what he was saying, he had approached the wardrobe without difficulty, probably because of the practice he had already had in bed, and was now trying to draw himself up against it. He wanted actually to open the door, actually to show himself and speak with the chief clerk; he was eager to learn what the others, who were now so desirous of his presence, would say when they saw him. If they got frightened, then Gregor would have no further responsibility and

The Metamorphosis

2 lively 元気 Be patient がまんしてください 3 for just another moment もうちょっとのあいだ I'm not quite as well yet as I thought 思ったほどは、まだ体調がよくない 4 The things that can affect a person 人間に影響を与えるいろんなことがある 6 it might be better to say (that 以下のように) いったほうがいいのかもしれない 7 a little advance indication ささやかな前兆 People should have noticed it みんなはそれに気づくべきだった（けれど、気づかなかった） 8 from the way I looked ぼくの様子から 10 fight off an illness 病気をやっつける 11 Spare 勘弁する basis 根拠、理由 13 no one has said a word to me about them だれもそんなことをぼくにいったことがない 14 the last orders こないだの注文書 17 in no time すぐに 18 please be good enough to tell them that どうか、(that、つまり I'll be at the office myself in no time と) みなさんにお伝えください give my best wishes よろしくと伝える

20 pouring all of this out こんなことをぺらぺらしゃべる 21 scarcely knowing ほとんどわかっていない 22 without difficulty 楽々と 23 because of the practice 練習のおかげで 24 draw himself up against it ワードローブにもたれるようにして立ち上がる 26 eager to learn 知りたい 27 desirous of his presence 彼に出てきてほしがっている 29 further responsibility これ以上の責任

could be calm. But if they accepted everything calmly, then he, too, would have no cause to be upset, and, if he hurried, he could really be at the station at eight o'clock. At first, now, he slid back down the smooth wardrobe several times, but finally, giving himself one last thrust, he stood there upright; he paid no more attention to the pains in his abdomen, severe as they were. Now he let himself fall against the backrest of a nearby chair and held tight to its edges with his little legs. By doing so, moreover, he had also gained control over himself and he fell silent, because now he could listen to the chief clerk.

"Did you understand even a single word?" the chief clerk was asking his parents; "he isn't trying to make a fool of us, is he?" "God forbid," called his mother, who was weeping by this time, "he may be seriously ill, and we're torturing him. Grete! Grete!" she then shouted. "Mother?" called his sister from the other side. They were communicating across Gregor's room. "You must go to the doctor's at once. Gregor is sick. Fetch the doctor fast. Did you hear Gregor speaking just now?" "That was an animal's voice," said the chief clerk, noticeably quietly in contrast to the mother's shouting. "Anna! Anna!" called the father through the hallway into the kitchen, clapping his hands, "get a locksmith right away!" And already the two girls were running down the hallway with rustling skirts — how had his sister gotten dressed so quickly? — and tore open the apartment door. There was no sound of the door closing; they

2 **cause to be upset** 動揺する原因、困る理由 4 **slid back down** すべって転ぶ 5 **thrust** ぐいと押すこと 7 **abdomen** 腹部 **severe as they were** (they は the pains) 痛みはかなりひどかったのだが **let himself fall against the backrest** 椅子の背もたれに体をあずけた 9 **held tight to its edges** 背もたれの縁にしっかりつかまった 10 **gained control over himself** 落ち着いた

13 **Did you understand even a single word?** ひとことでも理解できましたか？（グレーゴルの言葉のことをいっている） 14 **make a fool of us** わたしたちをばかにする 15 **God forbid** とんでもありません 16 **by this time** そのときにはもう 17 **torturing** 苦しめている **Grete** グレーテ（妹の名前） 19 **communicating across Gregor's room** グレーゴルの部屋をはさんだあちらとこちらで話をしている 20 **Fetch** 連れてくる 22 **noticeably** はっきりと 23 **in contrast to** 対照的に **Anna** アンナ（母親の名前） 24 **through the hallway into the kitchen** 玄関ホールのむこうからキッチンの中に 25 **locksmith** 錠前屋、鍵屋 26 **the two girls** ふたりの娘（おそらく妹と、ここで雇われている女の子） 27 **with rustling skirts** スカートの音をさせながら 28 **tore open** 勢いよく開ける

had most likely left it open, as is the case in apartments where a great misfortune has occurred.

But Gregor had become much calmer. To be sure, he now realized that his speech was no longer intelligible, even though it had seemed clear enough to him, clearer than before, perhaps because his ears were getting used to it. But anyway they were now believing that there was something wrong with him and they were ready to help him. The confidence and security with which the first measures had been taken, comforted him. He felt that he was once more drawn into the circle of humanity and hoped for magnificent and surprising achievements on the part of both, the doctor and the locksmith, without really differentiating much between them. In order to restore his voice to its maximum clarity for the imminent decisive discussions, he cleared it a little by coughing, but took care to do this in very muffled tones, since possibly even that noise might sound different from human coughing, and he no longer trusted himself to make the distinction. Meanwhile it had become completely quiet in the adjoining room. Perhaps his parents were sitting at the table with the chief clerk and whispering quietly, perhaps they were all leaning against the door and listening.

Gregor shoved himself slowly to the door, using the chair; once there, he let it go and threw himself against the door, holding himself upright against it — the balls of his little feet contained some sticky substance — and rested there from his exertions for the space of a minute.

1 **most likely** おそらく **left it open** 開けっ放しにしていった **as is the case** よくあること
4 **his speech was no longer intelligible** 自分の言葉がもう相手には理解できない 5 **even though it had seemed clear enough to him** しかし自分にはわかりやすいように思えた 6 **his ears were getting used to it** 耳が慣れてきている 8 **something wrong with him** 彼の調子がおかしい 9 **The confidence and security** 信頼できる確かさ **the first measures had been taken** 最初の処置がとられた 10 **comforted**（主語は The confidence and security）ほっとさせた 11 **the circle of humanity** 人の輪 12 **magnificent and surprising achievements** 立派で驚くべき仕事 13 **on the part of** 〜の側に 14 **differentiating** 区別する 15 **maximum clarity** 最大限の明瞭さ **imminent** 急を要する 16 **decisive** 決定的な **cleared it** はっきりさせた 17 **muffled** おさえた **since** なぜなら 18 **possibly** もしかしたら 19 **no longer** もはや〜でなくなる **make the distinction** 違いがわかる 20 **Meanwhile** 一方 21 **the adjoining room** 隣の部屋 22 **whispering quietly** 声をひそめて話している 23 **leaning against the door and listening** ドアにもたれかかって聞き耳を立てている

25 **shoved** 前に進んでいく **using the chair** 椅子を使って、椅子につかまって 26 **let it go** 椅子を放した **threw himself against the door** ドアにもたれた 27 **holding himself upright** まっすぐ立って **the balls of his little feet** 小さな足の先の丸い部分 28 **sticky substance** ねばねばしたもの 29 **exertions** 大変な作業 **for the space of a minute** 一分ほど、ほんの少しの間

But then he prepared to turn the key in the lock with his mouth. Unfortunately it seemed that he had no real teeth — what was he to grasp the key with? — but, instead, his jaws were actually pretty strong; with their help he did really get the key to move, paying no heed to the fact that he doubtless was doing himself some injury, because a brown fluid issued from his mouth, ran down over the key and dripped onto the floor. "Listen there," said the chief clerk in the adjoining room, "he's turning the key." That was a great encouragement for Gregor; but all of them should have called out to him, even his father and mother; "Go to it, Gregor!" they should have called, "keep at it, work on that lock!" And, imagining that they were all following his efforts in suspense, he bit recklessly into the key with all the strength he could muster. He danced around the lock, now here, now there, following the progress of the key as it turned; now he was keeping himself upright solely with his mouth, and, as the need arose, he either hung from the key or pushed it down again with the full weight of his body. The sharper sound of the lock, as it finally snapped back, woke Gregor up completely. With a sigh of relief he said to himself: "So then, I didn't need the locksmith," and he placed his head on the handle, in order to open the door all the way.

Since he had to open the door in this manner, he was still out of sight after it was already fairly wide open. First he had to turn his body slowly around one leaf of the double door, and very carefully at that, if he didn't

The Metamorphosis

1 **turn the key in the lock** 鍵穴に突っこんである鍵を回す
3 **what was he to grasp the key with?** 何で鍵をつかめばいいのか **instead** 歯がないかわりに 4 **pretty strong** とてもごつい **with their help** あごの助けをかりて 5 **paying no heed to the fact that** (that 以下の)ことは気にせずに 7 **brown fluid issued** 茶色の液体が出てきた **ran down over the key** 鍵を伝って 11 **should have called out to him** 彼に声援を送るべきだった（けれど、声援を送らなかった） 12 **Go to it** がんばれ 13 **keep at it** あきらめるな **work on that lock** 鍵を回せ 14 **in suspense** 気をもみながら、はらはらしながら 15 **bit recklessly into the key** 思い切って鍵をくわえた 16 **muster** 奮い起こす 17 **following the progress of the key** 鍵の動きに合わせて 18 **solely with his mouth** 自分の口だけで 19 **as the need arose** その必要が生じると 20 **with the full weight of his body** 全体重をかけて 22 **snapped back** 開いた 23 **So then** ということは 25 **open the door all the way** ドアを開くところまで開ける、大きく開ける

26 **Since** 〜なので **in this manner** こんな方法で 27 **fairly wide open** かなり大きく開いている 28 **one leaf of the double door** 両開きのドアの片方

want to fall squarely on his back right before entering the room. He was still occupied by that difficult maneuver and had no time to pay attention to anything else, when he heard the chief clerk utter a loud "Oh!" — it sounded like the wind howling — and now he saw him as well. He had been the closest to the door; now, pressing his hand against his open mouth, he stepped slowly backward as if driven away by some invisible force operating with uniform pressure. Gregor's mother — despite the presence of the chief clerk, she stood there with her hair still undone from the previous night and piled in a high, ruffled mass — first looked at his father with folded hands, then took two steps toward Gregor and collapsed in the midst of her petticoats, which billowed out all around her, her face completely lost to view and sunk on her chest. His father clenched his fist with a hostile expression, as if intending to push Gregor back into his room; then he looked around the parlor in uncertainty, shaded his eyes with his hands and wept so hard that it shook his powerful chest.

Gregor now refrained from entering the room; he stayed inside, leaning on the leaf of the door that was firmly latched, so that all that could be seen was half of his body and, above it, his head tilted to the side, with which he peered toward the others. Meanwhile it had become much brighter outside; clearly visible on the other side of the street was a section of the building situated opposite from them, endless, gray-black — it was a hospital — with its regularly placed windows harshly

1 squarely まともに on his back あおむけに right before entering the room 部屋に入る直前に 2 maneuver 作業 4 utter（声を）あげる 5 the wind howling 風の吠えるような音 he saw him as well グレーゴルにも事務長が見えた 6 pressing his hand against his open mouth 片手を開いた口に押し当てている 8 as if driven away 追いやられるかのように、押しやられるかのように by some invisible force 何か目に見えない力によって 9 operating with uniform pressure 一定の力が作用している 10 despite the presence of the chief clerk 事務長がいるのにもかかわらず 11 undone from the previous night 前の晩からほどいたままになっている 12 piled in a high, ruffled mass くしゃくしゃにもつれてふくれあがっている 13 with folded hands 手を組んで 14 collapsed へたりこむ、くずおれる in the midst of her petticoats ペチコート（スカート）の中に billowed out 外側に広がった 15 lost to view 見えない 16 sunk on her chest 胸にうずめている clenched his fist こぶしをにぎる 17 a hostile expression 敵をにらむような目（表情） intending to 〜しようとしている 18 the parlor 居間、リビング in uncertainty 不安そうに 19 shaded his eyes with his hands 両手で目をおおう

21 refrained from 〜を控えていた、〜しないでいた 23 firmly latched しっかりかんぬきがかかっている 24 tilted to the side 片側にかしげている 25 peered toward the others ほかの三人を見つめている 27 situated opposite from them 彼らの（通りを隔てて）向かいにある 28 endless どこまでも続く 29 regularly placed windows 同じ間隔で並ぶ窓 harshly piercing its facade 病院の建物の表側に無情な穴を開けている（ように見えた）

piercing its facade; the rain was still falling, but only in large drops that were individually visible and were literally flung down upon the ground one by one. An excessive number of breakfast dishes and utensils stood on the table, because for Gregor's father breakfast was the most important meal of the day and he would stretch it out for hours while reading a number of newspapers. On the wall precisely opposite hung a photograph of Gregor that dated from his military service, showing him as a lieutenant, hand on sword, with a carefree smile, demanding respect for his bearing and his uniform. The door to the hallway was open and, since the apartment door was open, too, there was a clear view all the way out onto the landing and the beginning of the downward staircase.

"Now," said Gregor, who was perfectly conscious of being the only one who had remained calm, "I'll get dressed right away, pack the sample case and catch the train. Is it all right, is it all right with you if I make the trip? Now, sir, you see that I'm not stubborn and I am glad to do my job; traveling is a nuisance, but without the traveling I couldn't live. Where are you off to, sir? To the office? Yes? Will you make an honest report of everything? There's a moment now and then when a man is incapable of working, but that's precisely the right moment to recall his past performance and to consider that, later on, when the obstacle is cleared away, he will surely work all the more diligently and with greater concentration. I am so deeply obligated to our employer,

2 **individually visible** ひと粒ひと粒が見える **literally** 文字どおり 3 **flung down** たたきつける **excessive number of** 非常に多くの 4 **utensils** 食器 6 **stretch it out** (it は朝食) 長々ととる 8 **precisely opposite** 真向かいの 9 **dated from** 〜のときの 10 **lieutenant** 中尉 **a carefree smile** くったくのない笑み **demanding respect** 尊敬を要求している（どうだといわんばかりに） 11 **bearing** 姿 **uniform** 軍服 13 **a clear view** よく見える **all the way out onto the landing and the beginning of the downward staircase** 階段の上がり口と、下りの階段が数段まですっかり（landing は「踊り場」ではなく「階段をあがったところ」）

16 **perfectly conscious** 完璧にわかっている 17 **remained calm** 冷静でいる 19 **is it all right with you**（ここの you は父親と母親） 20 **sir** 事務長に対する呼びかけ **stubborn** 頑固な 21 **nuisance** 大変、しんどい 22 **Where are you off to** どこへいくんですか？ 24 **now and then** ときどき 25 **incapable of working** 仕事ができない **precisely** まさに **the right moment** 絶好の機会 27 **the obstacle is cleared away** 障害がなくなったら 28 **all the more diligently** さらにいっそうまじめに 29 **obligated to our employer** 社長には感謝している

you know that very well. Besides, I have my parents and sister to worry about. I'm in a jam, but I'll work my way out of it. But don't make it harder for me than it already is. Speak up for me in the firm! A traveling salesman isn't well liked, I know. People think he makes a fortune and lives in clover. They have no particular reason to reflect on it and get over that prejudice. But you, sir, you have a better overview of the true state of affairs than the rest of the staff; in fact, speaking in all confidence, a better overview than our employer himself, who, in his role as entrepreneur, can easily be led to misjudge one of his employees. You are also well aware that a traveling salesman, who is away from the home office almost all year long, can thus easily fall victim to gossip, contingencies and groundless complaints that he's completely unable to defend himself against because he generally hears nothing about them; or else he finds out only when he has just come back from a trip, all worn out, and gets to feel the bad results at home, personally, when it's too late even to fathom the reasons for them. Sir, don't go away without saying a word to me that shows me that you agree with me even a little bit!"

But at Gregor's first words the chief clerk had already turned away, and only looked back at Gregor over his jerking shoulder, his lips pouting. And during Gregor's speech he didn't stand still for a minute, but, never losing sight of Gregor, retreated toward the door, very gradually, as if under a secret prohibition against leaving the room. By now he was in the hallway, and, from

₂ **in a jam** 窮地に陥っている、とても困っている **work my way out of it** 努力してそこから抜けだす ₃ **don't make it harder for me than it already is** 今よりつらいものにしないでほしい ₄ **Speak up for me** ぼくの味方をしてほしい ₅ **he makes a fortune** セールスマンはしっかりもうけている ₆ **lives in clover** ぜいたくに暮らしている **They have no particular reason** 彼らにはことさら (to 以下する) 理由がない **reflect on it** それについて考える ₇ **get over that prejudice** その偏見を改める ₈ **overview** 概観 **the true state of affairs** 本当の現状 ₉ **the rest of the staff** ほかの社員 **speaking in all confidence** 自信を持っていいますが ₁₀ **in his role as entrepreneur** 企業家という役割においては ₁₄ **fall victim** 犠牲になる **gossip, contingencies and groundless complaints** 悪いうわさや、不慮の出来事や、根拠のない不満 ₁₆ **defend himself against** 自分を弁護する ₁₇ **generally** たいがいにおいて ₁₈ **all worn out** 疲れ切って ₂₀ **fathom** 推し量る **the reasons for them** それらの理由 ₂₁ **don't go away without saying a word to me that** (that 以下のことを) いわないで帰らないでください、(that 以下のことを) いってから帰ってください ₂₂ **agree with** 同意する **even a little bit** 少しくらいは

₂₃ **But at Gregor's first words the chief clerk had already turned away** しかし、グレーゴルの最初の言葉で、事務長はすでに背を向けていた ₂₄ **over his jerking shoulder** すくめた肩ごしに ₂₅ **pouting** すぼめて ₂₆ **stand still** じっとしている **never losing sight of Gregor** グレーゴルから目を離さず ₂₇ **retreated** 後退する ₂₈ **as if under a secret prohibition against leaving the room** まるで秘かに、部屋を出てはいけないといわれているかのように ₂₉ **from the abrupt movement** その突然の動きをみれば (anyone might think へ続く)

the abrupt movement with which he finally withdrew his foot from the parlor, anyone might think he had just burnt the sole of it. But in the hallway he stretched out his right hand as far as it could go in the direction of the stairway, as if a truly superterrestrial deliverance were awaiting him there.

Gregor realized that it simply wouldn't do to let the chief clerk depart in that frame of mind, or else his position in the firm would be seriously endangered. His parents didn't understand things like that so well: in all those long years they had gained the conviction that Gregor was set up for life in this firm, and, besides, they were now so preoccupied by the troubles of the moment that they had lost track of all foresight. But Gregor possessed that foresight. The chief clerk must be retained, pacified, persuaded and finally won over; after all, the future of Gregor and his family depended on it! If only his sister were here! She was clever; she had already started to cry while Gregor was still lying calmly on his back. And surely the chief clerk, who was an admirer of women, would have let her manage him; she would have closed the parlor door and talked him out of his fears in the hallway. But his sister *wasn't* there, Gregor had to act on his own behalf. And without stopping to think that he was still completely unfamiliar with his own present powers of locomotion, without stopping to think that once again his oration had possibly — in fact, probably — not been understood, he let go of the leaf of the door; shoved himself through the opening; tried

₂ **think he had just burnt the sole of it** 足の裏を火傷したのだろうと思う ₅ **superterrestrial deliverance** 天の救い
₇ **it simply wouldn't do** まずい (it は to 以下) **let the chief clerk depart** 事務長をいかせる ₈ **in that frame of mind** 今の気持ちのままで **or else** さもなければ ₉ **be seriously endangered** かなり危うくなる ₁₀ **things like that** そういう事情 ₁₁ **had gained the conviction that** (that 以下のような) 確信を持つようになっていた ₁₂ **set up for life** 一生、仕事をする ₁₃ **preoccupied** 気を取られている **the troubles of the moment** 今の問題 ₁₄ **lost track of all foresight** 先のことなど頭にない ₁₅ **retained** 引き留められる ₁₆ **pacified** なだめられる **persuaded** 説得される **won over** 納得される、味方になる ₂₀ **admirer of women** 女性の崇拝者 ₂₁ **would have let her manage him** 妹になら説得されていた (だろう) ₂₂ **talked him out of his fears** 事務長に話して恐怖をしずめてくれた (だろう) ₂₄ **act on his own behalf** 自分のために行動する **stopping to think** 落ち着いて考える ₂₅ **unfamiliar with** よくわかっていない ₂₆ **present powers of locomotion** 現在の運動能力 ₂₇ **oration** 話、言葉 **possibly** もしかしたら、おそらく ₂₈ **let go** 放す ₂₉ **shoved himself** 体を押しこんだ

to reach the chief clerk, who was already clutching the railing on the landing with both hands in a ridiculous manner; but immediately, while seeking a support, fell down onto his numerous legs with a brief cry. Scarcely had that occurred when, for the first time that morning, he felt a sense of bodily comfort; his little legs had solid ground below them; they obeyed perfectly, as he noticed to his joy; in fact, they were eager to carry him wherever he wanted to go; and he now believed that a definitive cure for all his sorrow was immediately due. But at that very instant, rocking back and forth as he contained his forward propulsion for a moment, he had come very close to his mother, directly opposite her on the floor. Suddenly she leaped up into the air, even though she had seemed so totally lost to the world; she stretched out her arms wide, spread her fingers and shouted: "Help, for the love of God, help!" She kept her head lowered as if she wanted to get a better look at Gregor, but in contradiction to that, she ran backwards recklessly. Forgetting that the laid table was behind her, when she reached it she hastily sat down on it, as if absentmindedly, and seemed not to notice that alongside her the coffee was pouring onto the carpet in a thick stream out of the big overturned pot.

"Mother, Mother," Gregor said softly, looking up at her. For a moment he had completely forgotten about the chief clerk; on the other hand, seeing the flowing coffee, he couldn't resist snapping at the air with his jaws a few times. This made his mother scream again,

1 **clutching the railing** 手すりをつかんでいる 2 **in a ridiculous manner** 滑稽な格好で 3 **seeking a support** （グレーゴルは）支えをさがしながら 4 **with a brief cry** 短く叫んで **Scarcely had that occurred** そうなってすぐに 6 **bodily comfort** 体が楽になった感じ **solid ground** かたい床 7 **they obeyed perfectly** 脚は完全にいうことをきいた **as he noticed to his joy** 気がついてうれしくなった 8 **they were eager to** 脚は（to 以下）したがった 9 **definitive cure** 決定的な救い 10 **immediately due** すぐにやってくる **at that very instant** まさにそのとき 11 **rocking back and forth** 前後に揺れながら **contained his forward propulsion** 前進するのをやめた、止まった 14 **leaped up into the air** 飛びあがった 15 **lost to the world** 呆然としていた 18 **get a better look at Gregor** グレーゴルをよくみる **in contradiction to that** それと正反対に 19 **recklessly** 思いきり 20 **the laid table** 皿や食器が載っているテーブル 21 **on it** （it はテーブル） **absentminded** 呆然として 23 **in a thick stream** どぼどぼと 24 **overturned** ひっくり返った

27 **on the other hand** 他方で、そのくせ 28 **snapping at the air with his jaws** 空気にかみつくようなまねをする、口をぱくぱくさせる

dash away from the table and fall into the arms of his father, who hastened to receive her. But now Gregor had no time for his parents; the chief clerk was already on the staircase; his chin on the railing, he was still looking back for a last time. Gregor spurted forward, to be as sure as possible of catching up with him; the chief clerk must have had some foreboding, because he made a jump down several steps and disappeared; but he was still shouting "Aaaah!" — the sound filled the whole stairwell. Unfortunately this flight of the chief clerk now also seemed to confuse Gregor's father, who up to that point had been relatively composed: instead of running after the chief clerk himself or at least not obstructing Gregor in *his* pursuit, with his right hand he seized the chief clerk's walking stick, which the latter had left behind on a chair along with his hat and overcoat; with his left hand he gathered up a big newspaper from the table and, stamping his feet, began to drive Gregor back into his room by brandishing the walking stick and the paper. No plea of Gregor's helped; in fact, no plea was understood; no matter how humbly he turned his head, his father only stamped his feet harder. On the other side of the room his mother had torn open a window despite the cool weather, and, leaning out, was pressing her face into her hands far beyond the window frame. Between the street and the stairwell a strong draught was created, the window curtains flew up, the newspapers on the table rustled and a few sheets blew across the floor. Implacably the father urged him back, uttering hisses like

1 **dash away from the table** テーブルから飛び退く 2 **hastened to receive her** あわてて母親を抱きとめた 4 **his chin on the railing** あごを手すりに置いて 5 **for a last time** 最後に一度 **spurted forward** 前に飛び出した 6 **catching up with him** 事務長に追いつく 7 **foreboding** 予感 9 **the whole stairwell** 階段全体 10 **this flight** 逃走 11 **up to that point** そのときまでは 12 **relatively** 比較的 13 **obstructing** ふさぐ、邪魔する 14 **seized** つかんだ 15 **the latter** 後者（事務長） 18 **stamping his feet** 足を踏み鳴らして **drive Gregor back into his room** グレーゴルを彼の部屋に追い返す 19 **brandishing** 振りまわす 20 **plea** 嘆願 21 **humbly** 卑屈に **turned his head** 頭を回す 23 **had torn open a window** 窓を開けていた 24 **leaning out** 体を乗りだして **pressing her face into her hands** 両手に顔を押しつける 26 **draught** (= draft) 風 27 **flew up** 吹き上げられた 28 **rustled** かさかさ音を立てる **a few sheets** 数枚の新聞紙 **Implacably** 容赦なく 29 **hisses** しっしっ、という声

a savage. Gregor, however, had no practice in walking backwards, and, to tell the truth, it was very slow going for him. If Gregor had only been able to turn around, he would have been back in his room right away, but he was afraid of making his father impatient by such a time-consuming turn, and at every moment he was threatened by a fatal blow on the back or head from the stick in his father's hand. But finally Gregor had no other choice, because he observed with horror that, when walking backwards, he wasn't even able to keep in one direction; and so, with uninterrupted, anguished sidewise glances at his father, he began to turn around as quickly as he could, but nevertheless very slowly. Perhaps his father noticed his good will, because he didn't disturb him in this procedure but from time to time even conducted the rotary movement from a distance with the tip of his stick. If only his father had stopped that unbearable hissing! It made Gregor lose his head altogether. He was almost completely turned around when, constantly on the alert for that hissing, he made a mistake and turned himself back again a little. But when at last he had happily brought his head around to the opening in the doorway, it turned out that his body was too wide to get through without further difficulty. Naturally, in his present mood it didn't even remotely occur to his father to open the other leaf of the door in order to create an adequate passageway for Gregor. His idée fixe was merely that Gregor was to get into his room as quickly as possible. Nor would he ever have allowed

The Metamorphosis

1 **a savage** 不作法な人　**had no practice in walking backwards** 後ろに歩く練習はしていなかった　2 **to tell the truth** じつのところ、実際　**very slow going** その進み具合はとても遅かった　3 **turn around** くるりと背を向ける　5 **making his father impatient** 父親をいらいらさせる　6 **a time-consuming turn** 時間のかかる方向転換　7 **a fatal blow** 強烈な一撃　**on the back or head** 背中か頭への　8 **had no other choice** ほかに選択肢はなくなった　9 **observed with horror that** (that以下のことに) 気づいてぞっとした　10 **keep in one direction** 一定方向に進む　11 **uninterrupted, anguished sidewise glances** じっと、困ったように横目でみること　13 **nevertheless** それにもかかわらず　15 **disturb him in this procedure** この動作の邪魔をする　16 **conducted the rotary movement** 方向転換を指揮する、助ける　**from a distance** 離れたところから　17 **If only** 〜してくれたらいいのに　18 **unbearable hissing** しっしっという、耐えられない声　**lose his head** 正気を失う　20 **on the alert** 警戒しながら　21 **turned himself back again a little** 少しもとにもどる　22 **brought his head around to the opening in the doorway** 頭を、開いているドアのほうに向けた　23 **it turned out that** (that以下のことが) 明らかになった　24 **get through without further difficulty** さらなる困難なしにドアを抜ける　25 **in his present mood** 父親の現在の不機嫌な状態では　**remotely** かすかにでも　**occur** 頭に浮かぶ　27 **an adequate passageway** 適当な（十分に広い）空間　**idée fixe** 固定観念　29 **Nor would he ever have allowed** 父親は許さないだろう

59

the circumstantial preparations that were necessary for Gregor to hoist himself upright and perhaps get through the door in that way. Instead, as if there were no obstacle, he was now driving Gregor forward and making a lot of noise about it; what Gregor now heard behind him was no longer anything like the voice of merely one father; it was really no longer a joking matter, and Gregor squeezed into the doorway, no matter what the consequences. One side of his body lifted itself up; he was lying obliquely in the opening; one of his sides was completely abraded; ugly stains were left on the white door; now he was stuck tight and wouldn't have been able to stir from the spot; on one side his little legs were hanging up in the air and trembling, those on the other side were painfully crushed on the ground — then his father gave him a strong push from behind that was a truly liberating one, and, bleeding profusely, he sailed far into his room. Next, the door was slammed shut with the stick, then all was finally quiet.

II

It was only at twilight that Gregor awoke from his deep, swoonlike sleep. He would surely have awakened not much later even if there had been no disturbance, because he felt sufficiently rested and refreshed by sleep, but it seemed to him as if he had been aroused by a hasty footfall and a cautious locking of the door that led to the hallway. The light of the electric street lamps

1 **circumstantial preparations** 状況にふさわしい準備　2 **hoist himself** 立つ　3 **Instead** それどころか　6 **was no longer anything like the voice of merely one father** 父親ひとりの声だけのようには思えなかった　7 **a joking matter** 冗談　8 **squeezed into the doorway** ドアの開いているところに体をねじこんだ　9 **One side of his body lifted itself up** 体の片側が持ち上がった　10 **obliquely** 斜めに　**one of his sides** 片方のわき腹　11 **abraded** すりむいた　**ugly stains** きたならしいしみ　12 **stuck tight** はさまってしまった　13 **stir** 身動きする　**from the spot** その場から　14 **those** (= his little legs)　15 **crushed** 押しつけられている　17 **liberating one** 解放してくれる一押し (one = push)　**bleeding profusely** かなりの血を流しながら　**sailed far into his room** 部屋の奥まで飛んでいった　18 **was slammed shut** 乱暴に閉められた

II

23 **It was...that** (It was...that の強調構文)　**twilight** 夕暮れ　24 **swoonlike** 気絶状態に似た　25 **even if there had been no disturbance** ほかの邪魔がなくても　27 **been aroused** 目覚めさせられた　**by a hasty footfall and a cautious locking of the door** せわしい足音と、こっそりドアに鍵をかける音

lay pallidly here and there on the ceiling and on the upper parts of the furniture, but down where Gregor was, it was dark. Slowly, still feeling his way clumsily with his antennae, which he was just now beginning to appreciate, he heaved himself over to the door to see what had happened there. His left side seemed to be one long scar, with an unpleasant tightness to it, and he actually had to limp on his two rows of legs. In addition, one leg had been severely damaged during the morning's events — it was a almost a miracle that only one had been damaged — and now dragged after him lifelessly.

It was only when he had reached the door that he noticed what had really lured him there; it was the aroma of something edible. For a basin stood there, filled with milk in which little slices of white bread were floating. He could almost have laughed for joy, because he was even hungrier than in the morning, and immediately he plunged his head into the milk almost over his eyes. But soon he pulled it out again in disappointment; it was not only that eating caused him difficulties because of his tender left side — and he could eat only when his whole body participated, puffing away — on top of that, he didn't at all like the milk, which was formerly his favorite beverage and which therefore had surely been placed there by his sister for that very reason; in fact, he turned away from the basin almost with repugnance and crept back to the center of the room.

In the parlor, as Gregor saw through the crack in the door, the gas was lit, but, whereas usually at that time

1 pallidly 青白く 2 down where Gregor was 下の、グレーゴルのいるところでは 3 feeling his way 行く手をさぐる clumsily with his antennae 触角を使って不器用に 4 appreciate (触角があることを) ありがたく思う 5 heaved himself 体を押すように進んだ 6 His left side seemed to be one long scar 左のわき腹が一本の長い傷のように感じられる 7 an unpleasant tightness 不快なひきつり 8 limp 足を引きずるようにして歩く 11 dragged after him 後ろに引きずっている lifelessly 死んでいるように

12 It was...that (It was...that の強調構文) 13 lured 興味を引いた aroma におい 14 edible 食べられる basin 洗面器 17 immediately すぐに 18 plunged his head 頭を突っこむ over his eyes 目の上まで 19 in disappointment がっかりして 20 eating caused him difficulties 食べることが困難だった 21 tender 痛む his whole body participated 全身を使った 22 puffing away がぶ飲みするように食べる on top of that そのうえ 24 beverage 飲み物 therefore だからこそ 25 for that very reason その理由 (彼が好きだからという理由) のために turned away 顔をそむける 26 repugnance 嫌悪感 crept back はってもどる

28 the crack すき間 29 the gas ガス灯

of day his father was accustomed to read his afternoon paper to his mother, and sometimes his sister, in a loud voice, now there was not a sound to be heard. Maybe that practice of reading aloud, which his sister always told and wrote him about, had fallen out of use recently. But it was so quiet all around, too, even though the apartment was surely not empty. "What a quiet life the family leads," Gregor said to himself, and while he stared ahead into the darkness, he felt very proud of himself for having been able to provide his parents and sister with a life like that, in such a beautiful apartment. But what if now all the peace, all the prosperity, all the contentment were to come to a fearful end? In order not to give way to such thoughts, Gregor preferred to start moving, and he crawled back and forth in the room.

Once during the long evening one of the side doors, and once the other one, was opened a tiny crack and swiftly shut again; someone had probably needed to come in but was too disinclined to do so. Now Gregor came to a halt directly in front of the parlor door, determined to bring in the hesitant visitor in some way or another, or else at least find out who it was; but the door wasn't opened again and Gregor waited in vain. That morning, when the doors were locked, they had all wanted to come into his room; now, after he had himself opened one door and the others had obviously been opened during the day, no one came any longer, and, in addition, the keys were now on the outside.

It wasn't until late at night that the light in the parlor

The Metamorphosis

1 **was accustomed to** 習慣になっていた **afternoon paper** 夕刊 3 **was not a sound to be heard** 物音ひとつきこえない 4 **which his sister always told and wrote him about** そのこと（父親が新聞を読んできかせること）を、妹は彼（グレーゴル）にいつも話したり、手紙に書いたりしていた 5 **had fallen out of use** 行わなくなった 10 **provide A with B** AにBを提供する 12 **what if...?** (if以下のようになったら)どうする、どうなる？ 13 **contentment** 満足 **come to a fearful end** 恐ろしい終わりを迎える **In order not to give way to such thoughts** そんな考えに屈しないように、そんなことを考えないように 14 **Gregor preferred to start moving** 動き始めることを選んだ 17 **once the other one** 一度、もう片方のドアも 19 **disinclined** 気が進まなかった 20 **came to a halt** 止まった 21 **bring in** 中に入れる **the hesitant visitor** ためらっている訪問者 **in some way or another** なんとかして 22 **or else** そうでなければ **at least** せめて 23 **waited in vain** 待ったがむだだった 27 **in addition** おまけに 28 **the keys were now on the outside** すべての鍵は外側（向こう側）から突っこんである 29 **It wasn't until late at night that...** 夜遅くになってやっと……

65

was turned off, and now it was easy to ascertain that his parents and sister had been up all that time, because, as could clearly be heard, all three now stole away on tiptoe. Surely no one would come into Gregor's room any more before morning, and so he had plenty of time in which to think without disturbance about how he should now reorganize his life. But the high, open room, in which he was compelled to lie flat on the floor, filled him with anguish, although he couldn't discover the reason for it, because, after all, it was the room he had occupied for five years — and, making a semiconscious turn, not without a slight feeling of shame, he dashed under the couch, where, even though his back was a little squeezed and he could no longer lift his head, he immediately felt quite comfortable, only regretting that his body was too wide to fit under the couch completely.

There he remained the whole night, which he spent partly in a half-slumber, from which he was startled awake time and again by hunger, and partly in worries and ill-defined hopes, all of which led to the conclusion that for the time being he had to stay calm and, by exercising patience and being as considerate as possible to his family, make bearable the unpleasantness that he was absolutely compelled to cause them in his present condition.

By the early morning, when the night had barely passed, Gregor had the opportunity to test the strength of his newly made resolutions, because his sister, almost fully dressed, opened the door from the hallway side

1 **was turned off** スイッチが切られた　**ascertain** 確かめる
2 **up** 起きている　3 **as could clearly be heard** はっきりきこえたのだが　**stole away** こっそり立ち去る　**on tiptoe** つま先立ちで　4 **Surely** きっと　6 **in which** たっぷりある時間の中で **without disturbance** 邪魔なしで、ひとりでゆっくり　7 **reorganize his life** 生活を再構築する、立て直す　**high** 天井が高い **open** 広々とした　8 **was compelled** 強いられていた　**lie flat** はらばいになる　**filled him with anguish** 彼を苦しいような気持ちにさせた　11 **making a semiconscious turn** はっきりと意識しないまま向きを変えて　12 **not without a slight feeling of shame** 気恥ずかしい気持ちがないでもなく　14 **squeezed** 背中がつかえる

18 **half-slumber** 浅い眠り　**was startled awake** はっとして目が覚める　19 **time and again** ときどき　20 **ill-defined hopes** はっきりしない希望、あいまいな希望　21 **for the time being** しばらく　22 **exercising patience** 我慢すること　**considerate** 思いやる　23 **make bearable** 耐えられるものにする　24 **was absolutely compelled** いやおうなく強いられている　**cause them** (the unpleasantness) 家族に（不快な思いを）させる
26 **when the night had barely passed** 夜が明けるか明けないころ　28 **newly made resolutions** 新たな決意　29 **fully dressed** ちゃんと服を着た、きちんと着替えた

and looked in uneasily. She didn't catch sight of him at once, but when she noticed him under the couch — God, he had to be somewhere, he couldn't have flown away — she received such a fright that, unable to control herself, she slammed the door again from outside. But, as if regretting her behavior, she immediately opened the door again and walked in on tiptoe as if she were visiting a seriously ill person or even a stranger. Gregor had moved his head out almost to the edge of the couch, and was observing her. Would she notice that he had left the milk standing, and by no means because he wasn't hungry, and would she bring some other food that suited him better? If she didn't do so of her own accord, he would rather starve to death than call it to her attention, even though in reality he had a tremendous urge to shoot out from under the couch, throw himself at his sister's feet and ask her for something good to eat. But his sister immediately noticed with surprise that the basin was still full, and that only a little milk had been spilled out of it all around; she picked it up at once, not with her bare hands, of course, but with a rag, and carried it out. Gregor was extremely curious to see what she would bring to replace it, and the most varied things came to mind. But he could never have guessed what his sister in her kindness actually did. In order to test his likings, she brought him a big selection, all spread out on an old newspaper. There were old, half-rotten vegetables; bones from their supper, coated with a white gravy that had solidified; a few raisins and almonds; a cheese

The Metamorphosis

1 **looked in uneasily** 不安そうにこちらをのぞいた **catch sight of** 気がつく、みつける   3 **he couldn't have flown away** 飛び去ってしまったはずはないのだから   4 **a fright** 恐怖   8 **a seriously ill person or even a stranger** 重症患者か赤の他人   11 **left the milk standing** ミルクを手つかずのままにしてある **by no means** 決して〜ではない   13 **suited him better** もっと彼に合った **of her own accord** 自分から   14 **starve to death** 飢え死にする **call it to her attention** 妹の注意をそれに向ける、妹にそのことをいう   15 **tremendous urge to shoot out** 飛び出したくてたまらない気持ち   21 **with a rag** 雑巾で   23 **to replace it** それの代わりにする **most varied things came to mind** 様々なものが頭に浮かんだ   25 **test his likings** 好みを試す   26 **a big selection** いろんな選択   28 **coated with a white gravy** ホワイトソースのかかった   29 **solidified** 固まった

that two days earlier Gregor would have considered inedible; a dry slice of bread, a slice of bread and butter, and a slice of salted bread and butter. In addition she set down the basin that had probably been designated permanently for Gregor; she had now poured water into it. And from a feeling of delicacy, since she knew Gregor wouldn't eat in her presence, she withdrew hastily and even turned the key in the lock so that Gregor would see he could make himself as comfortable as he wished. Gregor's little legs whirred as he now moved toward the food. Moreover, his wounds must have completely healed by this time; he felt no more hindrance. He was amazed at that, remembering how, more than a month earlier, he had cut his finger slightly with a knife and how that cut had still hurt him considerably even the day before yesterday. "Am I less sensitive now?" he thought, and was already greedily sucking on the cheese, which had attracted him immediately and imperatively more than any of the other foods. Quickly, one after the other, tears of contentment coming to his eyes, he devoured the cheese, the vegetables and the gravy; on the other hand, he didn't like the fresh food, he couldn't even endure its smell, and he went so far as to drag away to a little distance the things he wanted to eat. He was long finished with everything and was just lying lazily on the same spot when, as a sign that he should withdraw, his sister slowly turned the key. That startled him at once, even though he was almost drowsing by that time, and he hastened back under the couch. But it took

1 **two days earlier Gregor would have considered inedible** 二日前だったら、グレーゴルは、食べられないと思っただろう
4 **designated permanently for Gregor** グレーゴル専用にした
6 **from a feeling of delicacy** 気づかいから
9 **make himself as comfortable as he wished** グレーゴルがくつろいで食べられる（みられていると食べづらいだろうから）
10 **whirred** 細かく動いた
12 **hindrance** 支障
15 **still hurt him considerably** まだかなり痛かった
17 **greedily sucking** がつがつ食べる
18 **imperatively** いやおうなく
20 **tears of contentment** 満足の涙　**devoured** むさぼるように食べた
23 **went so far as to** (to 以下のような) ことまでした　**drag away** 引き離す
24 **was long finished with everything** ずいぶん前にすべて食べ終えた
26 **a sign that he should withdraw** 引っこんでいてちょうだい、という合図
27 **startled** びっくりさせる
28 **was almost drowsing** 眠りかけていた
29 **hastened back** あわててもどった　**it took enormous self-control to** (it は to 以下) 大きな自制心を必要とした

enormous self-control to stay under the couch for even the brief time his sister was in the room, because the hearty meal had swelled his body to some extent, and he could hardly breathe in that cramped space. In between brief bouts of asphyxia, with slightly protruding eyes he watched his unsuspecting sister sweep together with a broom not only the leftovers of what he had eaten, but even the foods Gregor hadn't touched at all, as if those too were no longer usable; and he saw how she hastily dropped everything into a bucket, which she closed with a wooden cover, and then carried everything out. She had scarcely turned around when Gregor moved out from under the couch, stretched and let himself expand.

In this manner Gregor received his food every day, once in the morning, while his parents and the maid were still asleep, and the second time after everyone's midday meal, because then his parents took a short nap and the maid was sent away by his sister on some errand. Surely *they* didn't want Gregor to starve, either, but perhaps they couldn't have endured the experience of his eating habits except through hearsay; perhaps his sister also wanted to spare them one more sorrow, though possibly only a small one, because they were really suffering enough as it was.

Gregor couldn't find out what excuses had been used on that first morning to get the doctor and the locksmith out of the apartment again, because the others, even his sister, not understanding him, had no idea that *he* could understand *them*; and so, when his sister was in

1 **for even the brief time** ほんの少しの時間でも　3 **hearty meal** 真心のこもった食べ物　**swelled** 膨らませた　**to some extent** かなり　4 **cramped space** 狭い場所　**In between brief bouts of asphyxia** 短時間の発作的窒息　5 **protruding eyes** 飛び出した目　6 **sweep together** 掃き集める　7 **broom** ほうき　**not only the leftovers of what he had eaten** 彼の食べ残しだけでなく　**but even the foods Gregor hadn't touched at all** 彼が手さえつけなかった食べ物まで　8 **as if those too were no longer usable** それら（手さえつけなかった食べ物）さえ、もう食べられないといわんばかりに　9 **hastily** さっさと　12 **turned around** 背を向ける　13 **let himself expand** 体を伸ばした

14 **In this manner** こんなふうに　17 **a short nap** 短い昼寝　18 **errand** お使い　20 **couldn't have endured** 耐えられなかった　21 **his eating habits** 食べ方　**except through hearsay** 話できく以外　22 **spare them one more sorrow** 両親をこれ以上悲しませないようにする　23 **though possibly only a small one** 小さな悲しみだけかもしれないけれど　24 **suffering enough as it was** 現状のままでも十分つらい

25 **excuses** 言い訳　26 **get the doctor and the locksmith out of the apartment** 医者と鍵屋にアパートから出ていってもらう　28 **had no idea that** (that 以下のことは）思ってもいなかった

his room, he had to content himself with hearing her occasional sighs and invocations of the saints. Only later, when they had gotten used to it all to some degree — naturally, their ever getting used to it altogether was out of the question — Gregor sometimes seized on a remark that was meant to be friendly or could be so interpreted. "He really liked it today," she said when Gregor had stowed away his food heartily, whereas, when the opposite was the case, which gradually occurred more and more frequently, she used to say almost sadly: "This time he didn't touch anything again."

But even though Gregor couldn't learn any news directly, he overheard many things from the adjoining rooms, and whenever the sound of voices reached him, he would immediately run to the appropriate door and press his whole body against it. Especially in the early days there was no conversation that didn't deal with him in some way, if only in secret. At every mealtime for two days he could hear discussions about how they should now behave; but between meals, as well, they spoke on the same subject, because there were at least two family members at home at any given time, since no one apparently wanted to stay home alone and yet the apartment could in no case be deserted altogether. Besides, on the very first day the servant — it was not quite clear what or how much she knew of the incident — had asked Gregor's mother on her knees to discharge her at once, and when she said good-bye fifteen minutes later, she thanked them tearfully for letting her go, as

The Metamorphosis

1 **had to content himself with hearing** きくことで満足しなくてはならなかった 2 **invocations of the saints** 聖人の名をとなえること 3 **to some degree** ある程度 4 **getting used to it altogether** それに完全に慣れること **out of the question** 問題外 5 **seized on a remark that** （that以下のような）言葉に飛びつく 6 **could be so interpreted** そう解釈できる 8 **stowed away** がつがつ食べる **whereas** それに対し **the opposite was the case** その逆のときには 9 **gradually occurred** 次第に起こるようになってきた

13 **adjoining rooms** 隣の部屋 15 **appropriate door** 目的に合ったドア、声のきこえるドア 17 **deal with him in some way** なんらかの意味で彼を扱っている 18 **if only in secret** こっそりとではあっても 20 **between meals, as well,** 食事のとき以外でも、同様に 22 **at any given time** いつも 23 **and yet** しかし 24 **in no case be deserted altogether** どんな場合でも、完全に留守にするわけにはいかない 26 **she** = the servant 27 **on her knees** ひざまずいて **discharge** 解雇する 29 **tearfully** 涙ながらに **letting her go** やめさせてくれたこと

if that were the greatest benefit they could confer upon her, and, without being asked to do so, swore a fearsome oath that she would never reveal the slightest thing to anyone.

Now Gregor's sister had to join their mother in doing the cooking; of course that didn't entail much effort because they ate practically nothing. Time and again Gregor heard them fruitlessly urge one another to eat, receiving no other answer than "Thanks, I've had enough" or the like. Maybe they didn't drink anything, either. Often his sister asked their father whether he wanted any beer, and offered lovingly to fetch it herself; then, as the father remained silent, she said, to overcome any reservations he might have, that she could also send the janitor's wife for it, but finally the father would utter a decided "No" and the matter was discussed no further.

Even in the course of the first day the father already laid their entire financial situation and prospects before both the mother and the sister. From time to time he got up from the table and took some document or some memorandum book out of his small Wertheim* safe, which he had held onto even after the collapse of his business five years earlier. He could be heard opening the complicated lock and closing it again after removing what he had been looking for. In part, these declarations by his father were the first heartening things Gregor had

---

* [An Austrian brand of safe widely used by businessmen at the time. — TRANSLATOR.]

The Metamorphosis

1 **benefit** ありがたいこと **confer upon her** 彼女にほどこす 2 **without being asked** 頼まれもしないのに **swore a fearsome oath** 恐ろしいほどの誓いを立てた 3 **reveal** 明かす、もらす

6 **entail** 必要とする 7 **Time and again** 何度も 8 **fruitlessly** 不毛なことに、むなしく 9 **receiving no other answer than** (than 以下のような) 返事しか受けとらない **I've had enough** もう十分、お腹はいっぱい 10 **the like** 似たようなこと **drink** 酒を飲む 12 **lovingly** やさしい気持ちから **fetch it** ビールを買ってくる 13 **overcome any reservations** 遠慮をさせないように 15 **the janitor's wife** 管理人の奥さん 16 **decided "No"** きっぱりとした「いらん」 **the matter was discussed no further** その件は、それ以上議論されなかった

17 **in the course of** 〜のうちに 18 **laid...before both the mother and the sister** 母親と妹に示した **their entire financial situation and prospects** 経済的な状況と、今後の見通し 19 **From time to time** ときどき 21 **memorandum book** メモ、覚え書き **Wertheim** オーストリアの金庫会社 **safe** 金庫 22 **held onto** 手放さないでおいた **collapse of his business** 倒産 23 **He could be heard...** 父親が〜する音がきこえた 24 **removing** 取りだす 25 **In part** いくぶん **declarations by his father** 父親による説明 26 **heartening** 元気づける、励ましになる

heard since his captivity. He had believed that his father had nothing at all left from that business — at least, his father had never told him anything to the contrary — and naturally Gregor hadn't asked him about it. Gregor's concern at the time had been to do everything in his power to make his family forget as quickly as possible the commercial disaster that had reduced them all to complete hopelessness. And so, at that time he had begun to work with extreme enthusiasm and almost overnight had changed from a junior clerk into a traveling salesman; as such, he naturally had many more possibilities of earning money, and his successful efforts were immediately transformed into cash in the form of commissions, cash that could be plunked down on the table at home before the eyes of his amazed and delighted family. Those had been good times and had never been repeated later, at least not so gloriously, even though Gregor subsequently earned so much money that he was enabled to shoulder the expenses of the entire family, and did so. They had grown used to it, the family as well as Gregor; they accepted the money gratefully, he handed it over gladly, but no particularly warm feelings were generated any longer. Only his sister had still remained close to Gregor all the same, and it was his secret plan — because, unlike Gregor, she dearly loved music and could play the violin soulfully — to send her to the conservatory the following year, regardless of the great expenses which that had to entail, and which would have to be made up for in some other way.

1 **since his captivity** 部屋から出られなくなって以来　3 **had never told him anything to the contrary** 彼に、その反対のことは何もいっていない　4 **naturally** 当然　5 **concern** 懸案事項、気にかけていたこと　7 **commercial disaster** 商売の破綻（破産）　**reduced** 状況を悪くする　9 **extreme enthusiasm** 度を超えた熱心さ　**almost overnight** ほぼひと晩のうちに　10 **junior clerk** 見習いの手人　11 **as such** a traveling salesman として　13 **transformed into cash** 現金になった　14 **form of commissions** 歩合制　**be plunked down** 放る　15 **amazed and delighted family** 驚き喜ぶ家族　17 **not so gloriously** それほど派手には　18 **subsequently** その後　19 **shoulder** 担う　20 **had grown used to it** それに慣れてしまった　23 **generated** 生じた　24 **remained close** 親しくしていた　**all the same** 以前と変わらず　**it was his secret plan...to** (it は to send her 以下)　25 **dearly** 心から　26 **soulfully** 情感をこめて　27 **conservatory** 音楽学校　**the following year** 来年　**regardless of the great expenses** 大きな出費になるにもかかわらず　29 **be made up for** 工面する　**in some other way** なんらかの手段で

Often during Gregor's brief sojourns in the city the conservatory was referred to in his conversations with his sister, but always merely as a lovely dream, which couldn't possibly come true, and their parents disliked hearing even those innocent references; but Gregor was planning it most resolutely and intended to make a formal announcement on Christmas Eve.

Thoughts like those, completely pointless in his present state, occupied his mind while he stood upright there, pasting his legs to the door and listening. Sometimes, out of total weariness, he could no longer listen and let his head knock carelessly against the door, but immediately held it firm again, because even the slight noise he had caused by doing so had been heard in the next room and had made everyone fall silent. "How he keeps carrying on!" his father would say after a pause, obviously looking toward the door, and only then was the interrupted conversation gradually resumed.

Because his father used to repeat himself frequently in his explanations — partly because he hadn't concerned himself with these things for some time, partly also because the mother didn't understand it all the first time — Gregor had full opportunity to ascertain that, despite all their misfortune, a sum of money, of course very small, was still left over from the old days and had grown somewhat in the interim, since the interest had never been touched. And, besides that, the money Gregor had brought home every month — he had kept only a few *gulden* for himself — had not been completely used

1 **sojourns** 滞在 2 **was referred to** 口に出された 3 **a lovely dream** かわいい夢 5 **innocent references** 無邪気な話 6 **resolutely** 絶対に **formal announcement** 正式な発表
8 **pointless** 無意味な 10 **pasting his legs to the door** 脚をドアにくっつけて 11 **out of total weariness** 完全にくたびれて 12 **let his head knock carelessly against the door** 不注意に頭をドアにぶつける 13 **held it firm again**（it = his head）頭をしっかり支えて、またぶつけたりしないようにする **the slight noise he had caused** グレーゴルが立てた音はどんなにかすかなものであっても 14 **doing so** 頭をぶつけたりすること 15 **How he keeps carrying on!** いったい、何をやってるんだ！ 16 **after a pause** しばらくして 17 **only then** そうなるとようやく 18 **interrupted conversation** 中断された会話
19 **repeat himself** 言葉をくり返す、説明をくり返す 20 **hadn't concerned himself** 関わってこなかった 21 **for some time** かなりの間 22 **the first time** 一回では 23 **ascertain** 確信する 26 **in the interim** その間に **interest** 利子 27 **been touched** 手を付けられている 29 **gulden** グルデン（お金の単位）

up and amounted to a small capital. Gregor, behind his door, nodded vigorously, delighted by this unexpected foresight and thrift. To tell the truth, with that surplus money he could have further reduced his father's debt to his boss, and the day when he could get rid of that job would have been much closer, but now it was without a doubt better the way his father had arranged it.

Now, this money was by no means sufficient for the family even to think of living off the interest; it might suffice to maintain the family for one or, at the most, two years, no more than that. It was thus merely a sum that should really not be drawn upon, but only kept in reserve for an emergency; money to live on had to be earned. Now, the father was a healthy man, to be sure, but old; he hadn't done any work for five years and in any case couldn't be expected to overexert himself; in those five years, which represented his first free time in a laborious though unsuccessful life, he had put on a lot of fat and had thus become pretty slow-moving. And was Gregor's old mother perhaps supposed to earn money now, a victim of asthma, for whom an excursion across the apartment was already cause for strain, and who spent every other day on the sofa by the open window gasping for breath? And was his sister supposed to earn money, at seventeen still a child whom one could hardly begrudge the way she had always lived up to now: dressing nicely, sleeping late, helping out in the house, enjoying a few modest amusements and, most of all, playing the violin? Whenever the conversation led

1 **a small capital** 多少の金額　3 **foresight and thrift** 慎重さと倹約　**surplus money** 余剰の　4 **reduced** 減らす　5 **get rid of that job** この仕事をやめる　7 **better the way his father had arranged it** 父親のとった方法のほうがよかった

8 **by no means** 絶対に〜ではない　9 **living off the interest** 利子で暮らしていく　10 **suffice** 十分である　**at the most** せいぜい　12 **be drawn upon** 頼る　13 **reserve for an emergency** まさかのときのためにとっておく　16 **overexert himself** 頑張りすぎる　17 **represented** 表す　18 **a laborious though unsuccessful life** 苦労を重ねたのに報われなかった人生　**put on a lot of fat** とても太った　20 **supposed to earn money** 金を稼がなくてはならなくなった　21 **a victim of asthma** 喘息の犠牲者　**an excursion across the apartment** アパートを歩きまわること　22 **cause for strain** 過労の原因　23 **every other day** 一日おきに　24 **gasping for breath** 息を吸おうとあえいで　26 **begrudge** いやがる　28 **modest amusements** ささやかな娯楽

to this necessity of earning money, Gregor would always first let go of the door and then throw himself onto the cool leather sofa located next to the door, because he was hot all over with shame and sorrow.

Often he would lie there all through the long nights, not sleeping for a minute but only scratching on the leather for hours on end. At other times he didn't spare the exertion of shoving a chair over to the window; he would then crawl up the ledge and, supporting himself against the chair, lean against the window, obviously only through some sort of recollection of the liberating feeling he always used to experience when looking out the window. Because, in reality, with each passing day his view of things at only a slight distance was becoming increasingly blurry; the hospital opposite, the all-too-frequent sight of which he used to curse, he now could no longer see at all, and if he hadn't been perfectly well aware that he lived on the tranquil but thoroughly urban Charlottenstrasse, he might have thought that what he saw from his window was a featureless solitude, in which the gray sky and the gray earth blended inseparably. His attentive sister had only needed to notice twice that the chair was standing by the window, and now, each time she had finished cleaning up the room, she shoved the chair right back to the window, and from that time on even left the inner casement open.

If Gregor had only been able to speak with his sister and thank her for all she had to do for him, he would have endured her services more easily; but, as it was,

2 **let go of the door** ドアから離れて
6 **scratching on the leather** （家具の）革を引っかきながら
7 **on end** 続けて、ずっと **didn't spare the exertion** 労力を惜しまなかった 8 **shoving** 押し出す 9 **crawl up the ledge** 椅子の横桟をよじ登る **supporting himself against the chair** 椅子で体を支えて 10 **lean against the window** 窓にもたれる 11 **through some sort of recollection** ある種の回想によって **the liberating feeling** 開放的な気分 13 **in reality** 実際 **with each passing day** 日に日に 14 **his view of things** ものの見え方 **at only a slight distance** ほんのすぐ近くでも 15 **blurry** ぼやける **the hospital opposite** 向かいの病院 **the all-too-frequent sight** しょっちゅうみること 16 **curse** 悪口をいう 18 **the tranquil but thoroughly urban** 静かだが都会のまん中にある 19 **Charlottenstrasse** シャルロッテ通り 20 **featureless solitude** とらえどころのない荒野、茫漠とした荒地 22 **attentive** やさしい 26 **from that time on** それ以後 **inner casement** 二重窓の内側の窓
28 **he would have endured her services more easily** 妹の世話に、もっと楽に甘えられただろう 29 **as it was** 実際はそうではなかったので

they made him suffer. Of course, his sister tried to soften the painfulness of the situation as much as possible, and as more and more time went by, she was naturally more successful at it, but with time Gregor, too, made a much keener analysis of everything. Her very entrance was terrible for him. The moment she walked in, without taking the time to close the door, even though she was otherwise most careful to spare everyone the sight of Gregor's room, she ran straight to the window and tore it open hastily, as if she were almost suffocating, and then remained a while at the window breathing deeply, no matter how cold it was. She frightened Gregor twice a day with that running and noise; during the whole time, he trembled under the couch, even though he knew perfectly well that she would surely have spared him that gladly if she had been at all capable of staying in a room containing Gregor with the window closed.

Once — probably a month had already elapsed since Gregor's transformation, and his sister should no longer have had any particular reason to be surprised at Gregor's appearance — she came a little earlier than usual and encountered Gregor while he was still looking out the window, motionless and posed there like some hideous scarecrow. It wouldn't have surprised Gregor if she hadn't stepped in, since by his location he was preventing her from opening the window at once; but not only did she not step in, she even jumped back and closed the door; a stranger might even have thought that Gregor had been lying in wait for her, intending

1 **suffer** 苦しめる 2 **painfulness of the situation** グレーゴルの置かれている状況のつらさ 4 **at it** (it は to soften the painfulness) 5 **keener analysis** いっそう鋭い分析 8 **otherwise** そうしなければ 9 **tore it open** 乱暴に開ける 10 **suffocating** 窒息する 13 **that running and noise** 妹が駆けこんでくる勢いと窓を開ける音 15 **would surely have spared him that** きっとグレーゴルにそんな思いをさせないようにしただろう 16 **gladly** 喜んで 17 **a room containing Gregor** グレーゴルのいる部屋

18 **elapsed** 過ぎた 20 **any particular reason to be surprised** ことさら驚くような理由 22 **encountered** 会った 24 **hideous scarecrow** おそろしいかかし（グレーゴルが窓にもたれかかっている姿） 25 **by his location** 彼がそこにいるせいで 27 **jumped back** 後ろに飛びのいた 28 **a stranger might even have thought that** 何も知らない人なら (that 以下のように) 考えただろう

to bite her. Naturally, Gregor immediately hid under the couch, but he had to wait until noon before his sister returned, and she seemed much more restless than usual. From this he realized that the sight of him was still unbearable for her and would surely remain unbearable for her in the future, and that she probably had to exercise terrific self-control not to run away at the sight of even the small portion of his body that protruded below the couch. To spare her even that sight, one day — he needed four hours for this task — he carried the bedsheet on his back over to the couch and draped it in such a way that he was now completely covered and his sister couldn't see him even when she bent down. If that sheet, in her opinion, hadn't been necessary, she could have removed it, because it was clear enough that it was no pleasure for Gregor to close himself off so completely; but she left the sheet where it was, and Gregor believed he caught a grateful look when he once cautiously raised the sheet a little with his head to see how his sister reacted to the new arrangement.

In the first two weeks his parents couldn't muster the courage to come into his room, and he often heard them expressing complete satisfaction with the work his sister was now doing, whereas up to that time they had frequently been vexed with his sister because she had seemed a rather good-for-nothing girl to them. But often now, both of them, the father and the mother, waited in front of Gregor's room while his sister was cleaning up in there, and the moment she came out she had to report

The Metamorphosis

3 **restless** 落ち着きがない、おどおどしている 4 **From this** そのことから 5 **unbearable** 耐えがたい 6 **in the future** これから先も 7 **exercise** はたらかせる **terrific** すごく大きな 8 **portion** 部分 **protruded** 突き出ている、はみだしている 9 **To spare her even that sight** その光景（はみだしている部分）さえ、妹にみえないようにするために 11 **draped** 上からかけた 13 **bent down** かがみこむ 14 **in her opinion** 妹の考えるところでは 16 **close himself off** 閉じこもってしまう 17 **left the sheet where it was** シーツをそこにあるままにした 18 **a grateful look** 感謝の表情

21 **muster the courage** 勇気をふるいおこす 23 **expressing** 口にしている 24 **up to that time** そのときまでは 25 **vexed** いらだっていた 26 **good-for-nothing girl** 役に立たない娘 29 **the moment**（接続詞）= as soon as

in detail on how the room looked, what Gregor had eaten, how he had behaved this time, and whether a slight improvement could perhaps be noticed. As it was, the mother wanted to visit Gregor relatively early on, but at first the father and the sister held her back with sensible reasons, which Gregor listened to most attentively, and which he fully concurred with. Later, however, she had to be restrained forcefully, and when she then called: "Let me in to Gregor; after all, he's my poor son! Don't you understand I must go to him?," Gregor thought it might be a good thing after all if his mother came in, not every day of course, but perhaps once a week; after all, she understood everything much better than his sister, who, despite all her spunk, was still only a child and, in the final analysis, had perhaps undertaken such a difficult task only out of childish thoughtlessness.

Gregor's wish to see his mother was soon fulfilled. During the day Gregor didn't want to show himself at the window, if only out of consideration for his parents, but he also couldn't crawl very much on the few square yards of the floor; even at night he found it difficult to lie still. Soon he no longer derived the slightest pleasure from eating, either, and so for amusement he acquired the habit of crawling in all directions across the walls and ceiling. He especially enjoyed hanging up on the ceiling; it was quite different from lying on the floor; one could breathe more easily; a mild vibration passed through his body; and in the almost happy forgetfulness that Gregor experienced up there, it sometimes hap-

The Metamorphosis

1 **in detail** 詳しく 3 **As it was** 実際のところ 4 **relatively early on** 比較的早いうちに 5 **sensible reasons** もっともな理由 7 **concurred** 同意した、もっともだと思った 8 **be restrained forcefully** 強制的に引き留められる 9 **after all** やはり、どうしたって 14 **despite all her spunk** 妹は元気（勇気）はあるものの 16 **out of childish thoughtlessness** 子どもっぽい考えのなさから

19 **out of consideration for his parents** 両親のことを考えて 22 **lie still** じっとしている **no longer derived** もはや得られなくなった 24 **crawling in all directions** あちこちはいまわる 25 **hanging up on the ceiling** 天井からぶら下がる 27 **one** (一般人称だが、グレーゴルのこと) **vibration** 揺れ **passed through his body** 全身を伝わる 28 **happy forgetfulness** 楽しくて忘れること

pened that to his own surprise he let go and crashed onto the floor. But now he naturally had much greater control over his body than before and even such a great fall did him no harm. Now, his sister immediately noticed this new diversion that Gregor had discovered for himself — even when crawling he left behind traces of his sticky substance here and there — and then she got the notion of enabling Gregor to crawl around as freely as possible, by removing the furniture that prevented this, especially the wardrobe and the desk. But she was unable to do this on her own; she didn't dare ask her father to help; the servant surely wouldn't have helped her, because even though this girl of about sixteen was sticking it out bravely since the previous cook had been discharged, she had nevertheless requested permission to keep the kitchen locked at all times and to open it only when specially called; thus the sister had no other choice than to fetch her mother while the father was away one day. And the mother approached with exclamations of excitement and joy, but fell silent at the door to Gregor's room. Naturally, the sister looked in first to see if everything in the room was in order; only then did she allow the mother to enter. Gregor had in extreme haste pulled the sheet even lower down, making more folds in it; the whole thing really looked like a sheet that had been thrown over the couch merely by chance. Also, this time Gregor refrained from peering out from under the sheet; he gave up the opportunity of seeing his mother this first time, in his happiness that she had finally come. "Come

1 **to his own surprise** 自分でも驚くことに **let go** 手や足を放す 2 **had much greater control over his body than before** 以前よりはるかに体を自由に動かせるようになった 5 **diversion** 気晴らし、遊び 6 **sticky substance**（体から出る）ねばねばしたもの 9 **removing** 取りのぞく 11 **on her own** 自分ひとりで **didn't dare ask her father** 父親に頼むことはできなかった 13 **sticking it out** 頑張っている 14 **had been discharged** やめてしまった 16 **only when specially called** 特別に呼ばれたときだけ 17 **thus** したがって **had no other choice than to**（to 以下する）以外になかった 18 **fetch** 連れてくる 19 **exclamations of excitement and joy** 興奮と喜びの大騒ぎ 22 **in order** 異常がない、いつも通り 23 **in extreme haste** 大急ぎで 24 **making more folds in it** いつもよりたくさんしわを寄せる 25 **the whole thing** 全体の概観 26 **by chance** たまたま 29 **his happiness that she had finally come** 母親がきてくれたという喜び

on, you can't see him," said the sister, and obviously she was leading the mother by the hand. Gregor now heard how the two weak women moved the old wardrobe, heavy as it was, from its place, and how the sister constantly undertook the greater part of the work, paying no heed to the warnings of the mother, who feared she would overexert herself. It took a very long time. After about a quarter-hour's work the mother said it would be better to leave the wardrobe where it was, because, for one thing, it was too heavy, they wouldn't get through before the father arrived, and, with the wardrobe in the middle of the room, they would leave Gregor no open path; and, secondly, it was not at all certain that Gregor would be pleased by the removal of the furniture. She thought the opposite was the case; the sight of the bare wall actually made her heart ache; and why shouldn't Gregor, too, feel the same way, since after all he was long accustomed to the furniture in his room and would thus feel isolated in the empty room? "And, besides, doesn't it seem," the mother concluded very quietly — throughout her speech she had been almost whispering, as if she wanted to keep Gregor, whose exact whereabouts she didn't know, from hearing even the sound of her voice (she was convinced he didn't understand the words) — "and doesn't it seem as if, by removing the furniture, we were showing that we have given up all hope for an improvement and were inconsiderately leaving him to his own resources? I think it would be best if we tried to keep the room in exactly the same condition

2 **leading the mother by the hand** 母親の手を引いている　3 **weak** 力の弱い　5 **undertook** 受け持った　**paying no heed** 注意を払わず、無視して　7 **overexert** 無理をする　9 **leave the wardrobe where it was** ワードローブをそのままにしておく　10 **get through** やりとげる　12 **no open path** 自由に動けなくなる　14 **She thought the opposite was the case** その逆だと思った　15 **the sight of the bare wall actually made her heart ache** ワードローブのなくなった壁をみると胸が痛んだ　16 **why shouldn't Gregor, too, feel the same way** グレーゴルも同じように感じるにちがいない　19 **feel isolated** 孤立してしまったように感じる　21 **throughout her speech** 話している間ずっと　22 **keep Gregor...from hearing** グレーゴルにきこえないようにする　**whereabouts** 居場所　24 **was convinced** 確信している　26 **all hope for an improvement** (グレーゴルの状態が) よくなるという希望すべて　27 **inconsiderately** 思いやりもなく　**leaving him to his own resources** 自分のことは自分でといわんばかりの状態にする

as before, so that when Gregor comes back to us again, he'll find everything unchanged and it will be easier for him to forget what happened in between."

On hearing these words of his mother's, Gregor realized that the lack of all direct human communication, together with the monotonous life in the midst of the family, must have confused his mind in the course of these two months, because he couldn't explain to himself otherwise how he could seriously have wished for his room to be emptied out. Did he really want to have the warm room, comfortably furnished with heirloom pieces, transformed into a cave, in which he would, of course, be able to crawl about freely in all directions, but at the cost of simultaneously forgetting his human past, quickly and totally? Even now he was close to forgetting it, and only his mother's voice, which he hadn't heard for some time, had awakened him to the fact. Nothing must be removed, everything must stay; he couldn't do without the beneficent effects of the furniture on his well-being; and if the furniture prevented him from going on with that mindless crawling around, that was no disadvantage, but a great asset.

Unfortunately, however, his sister was of a different opinion; not without some justification, true, she had grown accustomed to play herself up to her parents as a special expert whenever matters affecting Gregor were discussed; and so now, too, the mother's advice was cause enough for the sister to insist on the removal of not only the wardrobe and the desk, which were all

3 **what happened in between** それまでにあったこと
4 **On hearing** ～をきいて 6 **together with** ～とともに **monotonous** 単調な 7 **in the course of** ～のうちに 9 **otherwise** そうでなければ 11 **furnished with heirloom pieces** 家に伝わった家具を置いた 12 **transformed into a cave** (何もない) 洞窟に変えてもらう、変えられる 14 **at the cost of** ～を犠牲にして **simultaneously** 同時に 15 **close to forgetting it** それを忘れそうになっている 17 **had awakened him to the fact** 彼をその事実に気づかせた 19 **couldn't do without** ～なしではやっていけない **the beneficent effects** ありがたい効果 20 **his well-being** 彼の幸福 21 **mindless crawling around** 愚かにはいまわること 22 **disadvantage** 不都合、損失 **asset** 望ましいこと

24 **not without some justification** ある程度の理由がないわけではない 25 **play herself up to her parents as a special expert** 両親にたいして専門家のような役割を果たす 26 **matters affecting Gregor** グレーゴルに関する事柄 28 **cause** 理由 **insist on** 強く主張する

she had thought of at first, but all the furniture, except for the indispensable couch. Naturally, it was not only childish defiance and the self-confidence she had recently acquired so unexpectedly and with such great efforts, that determined her to make this demand; she had also made the real observation that Gregor needed a lot of space to crawl in, while on the other hand he didn't use the furniture in the least, from all one could see. But perhaps a further element was the romantic spirit of girls of her age, which seeks for satisfaction on every occasion, and by which Grete now let herself be tempted to make Gregor's situation even more frightful, so that she could do even more for him than hitherto — because nobody except Grete would ever dare to enter a space in which Gregor on his own dominated the bare walls.

And so she wouldn't let herself be dissuaded by her mother, who seemed unsure of herself, as well, in that room, out of sheer nervousness, and who soon fell silent, helping the sister move out the wardrobe with all her might. Now, in an emergency Gregor could still do without the wardrobe, but the desk — that had to stay. And no sooner had the women left the room with the wardrobe, which they were pushing while emitting groans, than Gregor thrust out his head from under the couch to see how he could intervene cautiously and with the greatest possible consideration for them. But, as bad luck would have it, it was his mother who came back first, while Grete in the adjoining room had her

2 **the indispensable couch** 必要不可欠な長椅子（ソファ）
3 **defiance** 挑戦　**self-confidence** 自信　4 **unexpectedly** 思いがけず　5 **determined her** 彼女に決意させた　6 **observation** 観察　8 **in the least** 少しも　**from all one could see**（one は一般人称だが妹のこと）彼女がみるかぎり　9 **a further element** さらにもうひとつの要素　10 **seeks for satisfaction** 満足を求める　**on every occasion** 機会があるたびに　11 **let herself be tempted to** 〜する誘惑にかられた　12 **frightful** ひどい　13 **could do even more for him than hitherto** これまで以上のことを彼にしてあげられる　15 **dominated the bare walls** なにもない壁を独り占めしている

17 **dissuaded** 思いとどまる　18 **seemed unsure of herself** 自信がなさそうにみえた　20 **with all her might** 一生懸命に　21 **an emergency** 緊急事態　22 **do** やっていく　23 **no sooner...than** (...) するとすぐに（than 以下）をした　24 **emitting groans** うめきながら　25 **thrust out** 突きだす　26 **intervene** 邪魔をする、ふたりを止める　27 **consideration** 思いやり　28 **as bad luck would have it** 運の悪いことに

arms around the wardrobe and was swinging it back and forth unaided, naturally without being able to move it from the spot. But the mother wasn't used to the sight of Gregor, which might make her sick, so in a panic Gregor hastened backwards up to the other end of the couch but could no longer prevent the sheet from stirring a little in front. That was enough to attract his mother's attention. She stopped in her tracks, stood still a moment and then went back to Grete.

Although Gregor told himself over and over that nothing unusual was going on, just a few pieces of furniture being moved around, he soon had to admit to himself that this walking to and fro by the women, their brief calls to each other and the scraping of the furniture on the floor affected him like a tremendous uproar, sustained on all sides; and, no matter how tightly he pulled in his head and legs and pressed his body all the way to the floor, he was irresistibly compelled to tell himself that he wouldn't be able to endure all of this very long. They were emptying out his room, taking away from him everything he was fond of; they had already carried out the wardrobe, which contained his fretsaw and other tools; now they were prying loose the desk, which had long been firmly entrenched in the floor, and at which he had done his homework when he was in business college, in secondary school and even back in primary school. At this point, he really had no more time for testing the good intentions of the two women, whose existence he had almost forgotten, anyway, because in

1 **swinging it** ワードロープを前後に揺らしていた 2 **unaided** だれの助けもなしで、ひとりで 3 **from the spot** その場から 4 **which** = the sight of Gregor **make her sick** 吐き気をもよおさせる、気分を悪くさせる 6 **stirring** 動いている 8 **in her tracks** 歩く途中で **stood still a moment** 一瞬かたまって
13 **this walking to and fro by the women** 母親と妹が歩きまわること 14 **scraping**（床を）こする音 15 **a tremendous uproar** すさまじい音 **sustained on all sides** まわり中に響く 17 **pressed his body...to the floor** 体を床に押しつけた **all the way** 思いきり、できるだけ 18 **irresistibly** いやおうなく 19 **all of this** こんなことすべてを 22 **fretsaw** 糸鋸 23 **prying loose** 揺り動かしている 24 **entrenched in the floor** 床に根が生えたようになっている 26 **secondary school** 中等学校 **primary school** 小学校 27 **At this point** この時点で 29 **in their state of exhaustion** 疲れ切っていたので

their state of exhaustion they were now working in silence, and only their heavy footfalls could be heard.

And so he broke out — at the moment, the women were leaning on the desk in the adjoining room, to catch their breath a little — he changed direction four times, not really knowing what he should rescue first; and then he saw hanging conspicuously on the now otherwise bare wall the picture of the lady dressed in nothing but furs. He crawled up to it in haste and pressed against the glass, which held him fast and felt good on his hot belly. That picture, at least, which Gregor was now completely covering, surely no one would now take away. He twisted his head around toward the door of the parlor in order to observe the women when they returned.

They hadn't allowed themselves much time to rest, and were now coming back; Grete had put her arm around her mother and was almost carrying her. "Well, what should we take now?" said Grete and looked around. Then her eyes met those of Gregor on the wall. It was probably only because her mother was there that she kept her composure; she lowered her face to her mother to keep her from looking around, and said, although tremblingly and without thinking: "Come, shouldn't we rather go back into the parlor for another minute?" Grete's intention was clear to Gregor; she wanted to lead her mother to safety and then chase him down off the wall. Well, just let her try! He sat there on his picture and wouldn't relinquish it. He would sooner jump onto Grete's face.

2 **heavy footfalls** 重い足音
3 **broke out** 飛び出した 4 **catch their breath** 息を整える
6 **rescue** 助け出す 7 **conspicuously** 目立っている **otherwise bare wall** そうでなければ（その絵がなければ）裸の状態の壁 8 **dressed in nothing but furs** 毛皮しかまとっていない 9 **pressed against the glass** ガラスに体を押しつけた
10 **which held him fast** ガラスが彼にぴったりくっついた
15 **They hadn't allowed themselves much time to rest** ふたりはあまり長いこと休まなかった 17 **almost carrying her** 母親を運んでいるような状態 19 **those of Gregor** グレーゴルの目
21 **she kept her composure** 妹は冷静さを失わなかった **lowered her face to her mother** 顔を母親の顔に近づけた 22 **to keep her from looking around** 母親にまわりをみさせないように 24 **for another minute** もうしばらく 25 **intention** 意図 26 **lead her mother to safety** 母親を安全なところに連れていく **chase him down off the wall** 彼を壁からどかす 27 **let her try!** やれるものなら、やらせてやろう！ 28 **relinquish** あきらめる **sooner** その前に

But Grete's words had been just what it took to upset her mother, who stepped to one side, caught sight of the gigantic brown spot on the flowered wallpaper, and, before she was actually aware that what she saw there was Gregor, called in a hoarse shout: "Oh, God, oh, God!" She then fell across the couch with outspread arms, as if giving up everything, and lay there perfectly still. "Just wait, Gregor!" called the sister with raised fist and piercing glances. Those were the first words she had addressed to him directly since the transformation. She ran into the adjoining room to fetch some medicine to revive her mother from her faint; Gregor wanted to help, too — there was still time to rescue the picture — but he was stuck tight to the glass and had to tear himself loose by force. Then he, too, ran into the adjoining room, as if he could give his sister some advice, as in the past; but he was forced to stand behind her idly. While she was rummaging among various little bottles, she got a fright when she turned around; a bottle fell on the floor and broke; a splinter wounded Gregor in the face, and some kind of corrosive medicine poured over him. Now, without waiting there any longer, Grete picked up as many bottles as she could hold and ran in to her mother with them, slamming the door shut with her foot. Gregor was now cut off from his mother, who was perhaps close to death, all on his account. He didn't dare open the door for fear of driving away his sister, who had to remain with their mother. Now there was nothing for him to do but wait; and oppressed by self-reproaches and worry,

The Metamorphosis

1 **what it took to upset her mother** 母親を不安にさせる要件だった、(グレーテの言葉は母親を不安にさせてしまった) 2 **caught sight of** 〜をみる **the gigantic brown spot** 大きな茶色いしみ (のようなもの) 4 **what she saw there** 彼女がそこでみたもの 5 **a hoarse shout** しゃがれ声の叫び 6 **fell across the couch** 長椅子に倒れた **with outspread arms** 両腕を広げて 7 **giving up everything** すべてをあきらめて 8 **raised fist** こぶしを振り上げて 9 **piercing glances** 刺し貫くような目 **addressed to him** 彼に向けて発した 12 **faint** 気絶 14 **stuck tight** ぴったりくっつく **tear himself loose** 体を引き剥がす 15 **by force** 力ずくで、無理やり 16 **as in the past** 以前のように 17 **idly** 何もしないで 18 **rummaging** かきまわす **got a fright** ぎょっとした 20 **a splinter** 瓶の破片がひとつ 21 **corrosive** 腐食性の 23 **with them** 瓶を持って 26 **on his account** 彼のせいで **didn't dare open the door** ドアを開けることができなかった 27 **for fear of driving away his sister** 妹を追いはらうようなことになってはいけないので 28 **nothing for him to do but wait** 彼は待つしかすることがない 29 **oppressed** 落ちこんだ **self-reproaches** 自分を責めること、自責の念

he began to crawl; he crawled all over everything, walls, furniture and ceiling, and finally, in his desperation, when the whole room was starting to spin around him, he fell onto the middle of the big table.

A brief while passed, Gregor lay there limply, it was quiet all around; maybe that was a good sign. Then the bell rang. Naturally, the servant was locked in her kitchen, and so Grete had to go open up. Her father had arrived. "What's happened?" were his first words; Grete's appearance had probably revealed everything to him. Grete answered in a muffled voice, probably pressing her face against her father's chest: "Mother fainted, but she's feeling better now. Gregor has broken loose." "I expected it," said the father, "I always told you so, but you women won't listen." It was clear to Gregor that his father had put a bad interpretation on Grete's excessively brief communication and assumed that Gregor had been guilty of some act of violence. Therefore Gregor now had to try to pacify his father, because he had neither the time nor the means to enlighten him. And so he sped away to the door of his room and pressed himself against it, so that when his father came in from the hallway he could immediately see that Gregor fully intended to return to his room at once, and that it was unnecessary to chase him back; instead, all they needed to do was to open the door, and he would disappear right away.

But his father was in no mood to observe such niceties; as soon as he walked in, he yelled "Ah!" in a tone

2 **in his desperation** やけになって　3 **spin** ぐるぐるまわる
5 **A brief while passed** しばらくして　**limply** ぐったりと
10 **Grete's appearance** グレーテの様子、状態　11 **muffled voice** くぐもった声、はっきりしない声　13 **has broken loose** 逃げだした、飛びだした　16 **bad interpretation** 間違った解釈 **excessively brief communication** あまりに短い話　19 **pacify** なだめる　20 **means** 手段　**enlighten** 真相をわからせる 21 **sped away** 飛んで行く　25 **instead** (chase him back) するかわりに　26 **right away** すぐに
28 **in no mood to** (to 以下のような) 気分ではない　**observe such niceties** 細かいことを考える　29 **in a tone that...both furious and happy at the same time** 激怒しながらもうれしそうな声で

that suggested he was both furious and happy at the same time. Gregor drew his head back from the door and lifted it toward his father. He hadn't really pictured his father the way he now stood there; recently, to be sure, he had been so occupied by the new sensation of crawling around that he had neglected to pay attention to events in the rest of the apartment, as he had done earlier; and he should really have been prepared to encounter altered circumstances. And yet, and yet, was this still his father? The same man who would lie wearily, buried in his bed, when Gregor used to "move out smartly" on a business trip; who had received him wearing a bathrobe and sitting in an armchair when he returned home in the evening; who hadn't been fully capable of standing up, and had merely raised his arms as a sign of joy; who, during their rare family strolls on a few Sundays of the year and on the major holidays, would walk between Gregor and his mother, who walked slowly even on their own, but would always be a little slower yet, bundled up in his old coat and working his way forward with his crook-handled stick always placed cautiously before him; who, when he wanted to say something, almost always came to a halt and gathered the rest of the group around him? Now, however, he was perfectly erect, dressed in a tight blue uniform with gold buttons, like those worn by messengers in banking houses. Above the high, stiff collar of the jacket his pronounced double chin unfurled; below his bushy eyebrows the gaze of his dark eyes shone brightly and

3 pictured 思い描いた 4 to be sure 確かに 5 occupied 頭がいっぱい sensation 快感 7 events in the rest of the apartment アパート内で起こっている出来事 8 should really have been prepared 準備すべきであった（準備していなかった） 9 encounter altered circumstances 変わってしまった状況に出会うこと And yet しかし 10 was this still his father? これがまだ本当に自分の父親なのか？ 11 wearily 疲れて "move out smartly"「さっそうと家を出る」 14 fully capable of standing up ちゃんと立つ 16 rare family strolls たまの家族での散歩 19 even on their own グレーゴルと母親だけのときでも 20 bundled up 包まれて working his way forward 前に進む 21 crook-handled stick 曲がった柄（握り）のついたステッキ 23 came to a halt 立ち止まった 24 the rest of the group 自分以外の家族 25 erect 背筋をのばして立っている 26 worn by messengers in banking houses 銀行で使い走りが着ているような 28 his pronounced double chin unfurled 二重あごをはっきりみせていた bushy eyebrows もじゃもじゃの眉

observantly; his usually tousled white hair was combed down flat and gleaming, with a painfully exact part. He threw his hat, which was adorned by a gold monogram, probably that of some bank, in an arc across the whole room onto the couch; and, pushing back the tails of his long uniform jacket, his hands in his trousers pockets, he walked toward Gregor with a morose expression. He most likely had no idea himself of what he intended to do; nevertheless, he raised his feet unusually high, and Gregor was amazed at the gigantic size of his boot soles. But he didn't dwell on that, for he had known ever since the first day of his new life that his father considered nothing but the greatest severity appropriate where he was concerned. And so he ran in front of his father, came to a halt when his father stood still and immediately sprinted forward if his father made any kind of move. In that way they circled the room several times, without anything decisive occurring; in fact, because of the slow tempo the whole thing didn't have the appearance of a pursuit. For that reason, as well, Gregor stayed on the floor for the time being, especially because he was afraid that his father might look upon a scurry onto the walls or ceiling as being particularly malicious. And yet Gregor had to tell himself that even the present activity would soon be too much for him, because for every step his father took he had to execute a huge number of movements. Shortness of breath was already becoming noticeable, and even in his earlier days his lungs hadn't been the most reliable. As he was now staggering along,

1 **observantly** 鋭く　**tousled** もつれている　**combed down flat** 櫛でぺったりなでつけられていた　2 **painfully** 入念に、きっちりと　3 **was adorned** 飾られていた　**monogram** 名前のイニシャルなどを図案化したもの　4 **in an arc** 放物線を描いて　**across the whole room** 部屋の端から端まで　5 **onto the couch** 長椅子の上に　**pushing back the tails** 端を押さえて　7 **a morose expression** むっつりした表情　10 **his boot soles** ブーツの靴底　11 **dwell on that** そのことを考える　**for** なぜなら　12 **considered nothing but the greatest severity appropriate** 最も厳しい態度こそが適切であると考えた（nothing but = only）　13 **severity** 厳しさ　**he was concerned** グレーゴルに対しては　16 **sprinted forward** 飛びだした　**made any kind of move** 少しでも動こうものなら　17 **circled the room** 部屋の中をぐるぐる回った　**without anything decisive occurring** 何ひとつ決定的なことは起こらないまま　20 **pursuit** 追いかけ　21 **for the time being** しばらく　22 **look upon A as B** AをBとみなす　**a scurry onto the walls or ceiling** 壁か天井にはいあがること　23 **malicious** 悪意がある　24 **the present activity** 現在の行動　25 **too much for him** 彼にとって大きな負担になる　**for every step his father took** 父親がひと足歩くごとに　26 **execute** 行う　29 **reliable** 頼りになる　**staggering** 足がふらつく

in order to gather all his strength for running, and could barely keep his eyes open — unable, in his dazed condition, to think of any other refuge than running, and almost forgetting that the walls were open to him (although in this room they were obstructed by painstakingly carved furniture full of prongs and points) — something that had been lightly tossed flew right by him and rolled in front of him on the floor. It was an apple; another flew at him immediately afterward; Gregor stood still in fright; to continue running was pointless, because his father had decided to bombard him. He had filled his pockets from the fruit bowl on the sideboard and now, without aiming carefully for the moment, was throwing one apple after another. A weakly thrown apple grazed Gregor's back, but rolled off harmlessly. One that flew right after it actually penetrated Gregor's back; Gregor wanted to drag himself onward, as if the surprising and unbelievable pain might pass if he changed location; but he felt pinned down and he surrendered, all his senses fully bewildered. It was only with his last glance that he still saw the door of his room being torn open; he saw his mother dash out ahead of his screaming sister (the mother was in her shift, because the sister had undressed her to make it easier for her to breathe when she had fainted); he then saw the mother run over to the father, her untied petticoats slipping to the floor one after the other as she went. Tripping over the petticoats, she rushed upon the father and, embracing him, in absolute union with him — at this point all went dark for Gregor

1 **gather all his strength** 全力を尽くして 2 **dazed condition** ぼんやりした状態 3 **refuge** 逃げ方 4 **walls were open** 壁が自由に使える状態である 5 **were obstructed** ふさがれていた **painstakingly carved furniture** とても細かい彫刻のほどこされた家具 6 **prongs and points** デコボコやギザギザ **something that had been lightly tossed** 軽く投げられた何か 7 **flew right by him** 彼のすぐそばまで飛んできた 10 **pointless** 無意味 11 **bombard** (リンゴで) 砲撃する 12 **sideboard** サイドボード (食器台) 13 **for the moment** しばらくは 14 **grazed** かすめた 16 **penetrated** めりこんだ 17 **drag himself onward** 前にはっていく 18 **if he changed location** 場所を変えたら 19 **pinned down** 身動きできなくなった **surrendered** 降参した **senses** 感覚 20 **bewildered** うろたえた **It was...that** (It was...that の強調構文) 23 **shift** シュミーズ 26 **untied petticoats** 紐をほどいてあったペチコート 27 **Tripping** つまずきながら 28 **in absolute union with him** 夫との完全な一体化 29 **all went dark** 目の前がまっ暗になった

— with her hands behind the father's head, she begged him to spare Gregor's life.

III

Gregor's severe injury, from which he suffered for more than a month — since no one dared to remove the apple, it remained in his flesh as a visible reminder — seemed to have made even his father recall that, despite his present sad and disgusting shape, Gregor was a member of the family who shouldn't be treated as an enemy, but in whose case family obligations demanded that one swallow one's repulsion and be patient, only patient.

And even if Gregor's wound had probably impaired his mobility for good, and he now, like an old invalid, needed long, long minutes to cross his room — crawling up high was out of the question — he received in exchange for this worsening of his condition something he considered a perfectly adequate replacement: as every evening approached, the parlor door, which he would begin to watch carefully an hour or two ahead of time, was opened so that, lying in the dark, invisible from the parlor, he could see the whole family at the brightly lit table and listen to their conversation, to some extent with everyone's permission, and thus quite otherwise than before.

Of course, these were no longer the lively discussions of the old days, to which Gregor's thoughts had always

2 **spare Gregor's life** グレーゴルの命を助けてやる

III

6 **severe injury** 重い傷　8 **a visible reminder** 目にみえる形で記憶を呼び起こすもの　9 **recall** 思い出させる　12 **in whose case** このような場合　13 **one**（一般人称の one だが、この場合は、家族のこと）　**swallow**（前に should を補う）飲みこむ、抑える　**repulsion** 嫌悪

15 **impaired** そこなう　16 **his mobility** 動き　**for good** ずっと、永久に　**old invalid** 体の不自由な老人　18 **out of the question** 問題外　**received**（目的語は something）　**in exchange for** ～と交換で　19 **this worsening of his condition** こんなふうに体が悪くなること　20 **adequate replacement** ありがたい代わりのもの　22 **an hour or two ahead of time** 1、2 時間前から　24 **at the brightly lit table** 明るく照らされたテーブルについている　25 **to some extent** ある程度　26 **with everyone's permission** みんなの許可を得て　**quite otherwise than before** 以前とはまったくちがっている

29 **to which**（which の先行詞は the lively discussions）　**Gregor's thoughts** グレーゴルの思い

turned with some yearning in his tiny hotel rooms, when he had had to throw himself wearily into the damp bedclothes. Generally the talks were very quiet. Right after supper the father fell asleep in his chair; the mother and sister admonished each other to be quiet; the mother, leaning far forward under the light, sewed fine linen for a clothing store; the sister, who had taken work as a salesgirl, was learning stenography and French at night so that she might possibly get a better job some day. At times the father woke up and, as if he didn't even know he'd been sleeping, he said to the mother: "How long you've been sewing again today!" and went right back to sleep, while mother and sister smiled at each other wearily.

With a sort of obstinacy the father refused to take off his messenger's uniform even at home; and while his bathrobe hung unused on the hook, the father drowsed in his chair fully dressed, as if he were always ready to do his work and were awaiting his superior's orders even here. Consequently, despite all the mother and sister's care, the uniform, which hadn't been brand new at the outset, became less and less clean; and often for entire evenings Gregor would look at this garment, stained all over, but with constantly polished and gleaming gold buttons, in which the old man slept in great discomfort and yet peacefully.

The moment the clock struck ten, the mother tried to wake the father by addressing him softly and then tried to convince him to go to bed, because here he

1 turned 向く with some yearning 軽い憧れをもって when 小さなホテルの部屋にいたとき 3 Right after supper 夕食が終わるとすぐに 5 admonished 厳しく注意した 6 leaning far forward 深くかがみこんで fine linen 上等の肌着 8 stenography 速記 12 went right back to sleep すぐにまた寝た 15 With a sort of obstinacy ある種の頑固さのせいで 16 messenger's uniform 配達人の制服 17 unused 着られないまま drowsed うとうとした 19 his superior's orders 上司の命令、指示 20 Consequently その結果 21 care 気づかい brand new 真新しい at the outset 最初は 22 for entire evenings 夜の間ずっと 23 this garment 父親の制服 stained 汚れている 25 in which（which の先行詞は this garment）
28 addressing 話しかけること 29 convince 納得させる

couldn't get any proper sleep, which the father needed very badly, since he had to begin work at six. But with the obstinacy that had taken hold of him since he had become a messenger, he constantly insisted on remaining longer at the table, although he regularly fell asleep, and then, on top of that, could only be persuaded with the greatest difficulty to give up his chair for his bed. In this situation mother and sister might urge him over and over with little reminders, for periods of fifteen minutes at a time he would shake his head slowly, keep his eyes closed and refuse to stand up. The mother tugged at his sleeve and said sweet things in his ear, the sister would leave her task to help the mother, but this had no effect on the father. He merely sank more deeply into his chair. Only when the women seized him under his arms would he open his eyes, look now at the mother and now at the sister, and say: "This is living! This is the repose of my old age!" And, supported by the two women, he would get up, slowly and fussily, as if he were his own greatest burden, and would allow himself to be led to the door by the women; there he would wave them away and proceed on his own, while the mother hastily flung down her sewing things and the sister her pen in order to run after the father and continue to be of service to him.

In this overworked and overtired family, who had time to be concerned about Gregor beyond what was absolutely necessary? There were constant retrenchments in their way of living; they finally had to let the servant

1 **needed very badly** とても必要としている 3 **had taken hold of him** 父親をつかまえている、支配している 6 **on top of that** そのうえ 7 **give up his chair for his bed** 椅子から立ち上がってベッドにいくこと 8 **urge** せっつく 9 **little reminders** (寝る時間だということを) 思い出させる短い言葉 11 **tugged at his sleeve** 父親の袖を引っぱった 13 **leave her task** 自分のやっていることを中断する 17 **This is living!** 人生とはこういうもんだ！ **the repose** 休息 19 **fussily** ぶつぶついいながら **as if he were his own greatest burden** 自分こそが自分の最もでっかい重荷だといわんばかりに 21 **wave them away** 手を振ってふたりを行かせる 22 **proceed on his own** ひとりで歩いていく **flung down** 放り出した 24 **be of service to him** 父親に手を貸そうと

27 **be concerned** 気づかう **beyond what was absolutely necessary** 絶対必要なこと以上に 28 **retrenchments** 解約すること 29 **in their way of living** 生活全般における

go; a gigantic, bony cleaning woman with white hair fluttering around her head now came in the morning and evening to do the heaviest chores; everything else was attended to by the mother, who also had all that sewing to do. It even came to pass that various pieces of family jewelry, which the mother and sister had formerly worn at parties and on great occasions, were sold, as Gregor learned in the evening from the family's discussion of the prices they had received. But the greatest complaint always was that they couldn't leave this apartment, which was far too big for their present means, since no one could figure out how to move Gregor. But Gregor realized that it was not only the concern for him that prevented a move, because after all he could easily have been shipped in a suitable crate with a few air holes; what principally kept the family from changing apartments was rather the complete hopelessness of the situation and the thought that they had been afflicted with a misfortune unlike any other in their entire circle of relatives and acquaintances. They were performing to the hilt all that the world demands of poor people: the father carried in breakfast for the junior bank clerks, the mother sacrificed herself for the linen of strangers, the sister ran back and forth behind her counter at the customers' command, but by this time the family's strength was taxed to the limit. And the sore on his back began to hurt Gregor all over again when, after putting his father to bed, his mother and sister came back, let their work rest, moved close together and sat cheek to cheek; when

1 **go** やめる **gigantic, bony** とても大柄で、骨太の 2 **fluttering** 振り乱して 3 **chores** 日常的な用事、雑用 5 **It** (It は that 以下) **even came to pass** 起こりさえした 11 **which was far too big**（which の先行詞は this apartment） **present means** 今の収入、財力 12 **figure out** 考えだす 14 **prevented a move** 引っ越しを妨げていた 15 **shipped** 送られた（だろう） **a suitable crate** ふさわしい箱 17 **the complete hopelessness** この完全な絶望状態 18 **afflicted** 悩まされている 19 **any other** ほかの人 20 **to the hilt** 剣の柄まで、どっぷり 21 **the world demands of poor people** 世間が貧しい人びとに要求する（こと） 22 **carried in breakfast** 朝食を運んできた **the junior bank clerks** 若い銀行員 23 **for the linen of strangers** 他人の肌着 24 **at the customers' command** 客にいわれて 26 **was taxed to the limit** 限界まで負担がかかっていた **the sore** 痛み 28 **let their work rest** 仕事を置いて 29 **cheek to cheek** 頬と頬を寄せて

the mother, pointing to Gregor's room, now said, "Close the door there, Grete," and Gregor was again in the dark, while in the next room the women wept together or just stared at the table with dry eyes.

Gregor spent the nights and days almost completely without sleep. Sometimes he thought that, the next time the door opened, he would once again take charge of the family's problems just as he used to; in his thoughts there reappeared, after a long interval, his boss and the chief clerk, the clerks and the apprentices, the office messenger who was so dense, two or three friends from other firms, a chambermaid in a provincial hotel (a charming, fleeting recollection), a cashier in a hat shop whom he had courted seriously but too slowly — they all appeared, mingling with strangers or people he'd forgotten, but instead of helping him and his family, they were all inaccessible, and he was glad when they disappeared. But at other times he was no longer at all in the mood to worry about his family; he was filled with nothing but rage over how badly he was looked after; and even though he couldn't imagine anything he might have had an appetite for, he laid plans for getting into the pantry so he could take what was still his by rights, even if he wasn't hungry. No longer reflecting about what might give Gregor some special pleasure, his sister now hastily shoved any old food into Gregor's room with her foot before running off to work in the morning and at noon; in the evening, not caring whether the food had perhaps been just merely tasted or — most frequently

7 **take charge of the family's problems** 家族の抱えている問題を引き受ける　8 **just as he used to** ちょうど以前のように　9 **after a long interval** 久しぶりに　10 **the apprentices** 見習い　11 **dense** 頭の悪い　12 **other firms** ほかの会社　**a chambermaid** メイド　**provincial** 田舎の　13 **fleeting recollection** はかない思い出　14 **had courted** 求婚したことがあった　15 **mingling with** 〜に混じって　16 **instead of** 〜しないで　17 **inaccessible** 近づきがたい　20 **rage over** 〜に対する怒り　21 **even though he couldn't imagine anything**（anything以下のようなものは）何も思いつかないにもかかわらず　**he might have had an appetite for** 自分が食欲を感じるかもしれない　23 **the pantry** 食料保存室　**his by rights** 当然の権利として彼のもの　24 **No longer reflecting** もう考えることもなくなり　26 **shoved...with her foot** 足で押しこんだ　28 **not caring** 〜にかまわず

— left completely untouched, she would sweep it out with a swing of the broom. The cleaning of the room, which she now always took care of in the evening, was done at breakneck speed. Long trails of dirt lined the walls, here and there lay heaps of dust and filth. At first, when his sister arrived, Gregor would station himself at particularly glaring corners of that sort, thereby intending to reproach her to some degree. But he could have remained there for weeks on end without seeing any improvement in his sister; she saw the dirt just as well as he did, but she had simply made up her mind to leave it there. At the same time, with a touchiness that was quite new to her, and which had come over the whole family, she took care that the cleaning of Gregor's room should be reserved exclusively for her. On one occasion the mother had undertaken a thorough cleaning of Gregor's room, which she had only managed to do by using several buckets of water — the excessive dampness harmed Gregor, too, and he lay stretched out on the couch, embittered and motionless — but the mother didn't escape the penalty: the moment the sister noticed the change in Gregor's room in the evening, she ran into the parlor, highly insulted, and, despite the mother's imploringly uplifted hands, she broke into a crying jag that the parents — the father had naturally been frightened out of his chair — at first watched in amazement and helplessness until they themselves began to stir. To his right, the father reproached the mother for not leaving the cleaning of Gregor's room to the sister; to his left, on

The Metamorphosis

1 **sweep it out** 掃き出す 2 **with a swing of the broom** ほうきをひと掃きして 4 **at breakneck speed** 首の骨を折りそうなくらいの速さで、すごい速さで **trails of dirt** 汚れの跡 **lined** 筋になってついていた 5 **filth** 不潔な物 6 **station** 置く 7 **glaring corners** 目障りな隅 **of that sort** そういう種類の（汚れたり、ゴミがたまったりしている） 8 **to some degree** ある程度、ある意味 9 **weeks on end** 何週間も連続で 10 **as well as he did** 彼が目にしているのと同じように 12 **a touchiness** 神経質っぽさ 13 **new to her** 妹にはそれまでになかった 15 **reserved exclusively for her** 妹だけがすることになった 16 **thoroughly cleaning** 徹底的な掃除 18 **the excessive dampness** びしょ濡れになること 19 **stretched out** ぐったり横になる **embittered** むっとして 20 **escape the penalty** 罰を免れる 23 **highly insulted** （母親の越権行為に）とても怒って **imploringly uplifted hands** 嘆願するかのように上げた両手 24 **broke into** いきなり〜する **a crying jag** 激しく泣きじゃくること 25 **out of his chair** 椅子から転げ落ちる、飛びあがる 27 **stir** 動きだす、行動を起こす **To his right** 右にいる（母親に）向かって 29 **on the other hand** その一方で

125

the other hand, he yelled at the sister, saying she would never again be permitted to clean Gregor's room, while the mother tried to drag the father, who was beside himself with agitation, into the bedroom; the sister, shaken with sobs, belabored the table with her little fists; and Gregor hissed loudly with rage because it didn't occur to anyone to close the door and spare him that sight and that commotion.

But even if the sister, worn out by her job, had grown tired of caring for Gregor as before, still the mother would not have been compelled to take over for her, and Gregor wouldn't have needed to be neglected. Because the cleaning woman was now there. This elderly widow, who, thanks to her powerful frame, had probably endured the worst during her long life, had no real horror of Gregor. Without being in the least curious, she had once accidentally opened the door to Gregor's room; at the sight of Gregor, who, taken by surprise, began to run back and forth although no one was chasing him, she had stood still in amazement, her hands folded over her stomach. Since then she never failed to open the door a little for just a moment in the morning and evening and to look in at Gregor. At the beginning she even called him over with words she probably thought were friendly, such as "Come on over here, old dung beetle" or "Just look at the old dung beetle!" Gregor never responded to such calls, but remained motionless where he stood, as if the door had never been opened. But if, instead of letting this cleaning woman disturb him needlessly as

The Metamorphosis

1 **yelled** 怒鳴りつけた　3 **drag the father...into the bedroom** 父親を引っぱって、寝室に連れていこうとする　**beside himself** われを忘れている　4 **with agitation** 興奮して　5 **belabored** 叩いた　6 **hissed** シューという声をあげた　7 **spare him that sight and that commotion** そんな有様や騒動を彼にみせない

9 **worn out** 疲れはてて　11 **have been compelled to** 〜せざるをえない　**take over for her** 妹のしていたことを引き継ぐ　12 **be neglected** ないがしろにされる　13 **cleaning woman** 掃除婦　14 **powerful frame** がっしりした体格　**endured the worst** どんなにひどいことも耐えてきた　16 **Without being in the least curious** たいした興味もなく　18 **taken by surprise** びっくりして　20 **her hands folded over her stomach** 腹の上で手を組んで　21 **Since then** そのときからずっと　**never failed to** 必ず〜するようになった　24 **she probably thought**（この部分はカッコに入れて考えるとわかりやすい。次の were の主語は words）掃除婦はおそらく〜と考えていたのだろう　25 **dung beetle** 糞玉を作るコガネムシ　27 **such calls** そんな呼びかけ　29 **disturb him** グレーゴルにいやな思いをさせる　**as the fancy took her** 気まぐれにまかせて

the fancy took her, they had only given her orders to clean his room every day! Once, early in the morning — a heavy rain, perhaps already foretokening the coming spring, was beating on the window panes — when the cleaning woman began with her series of expressions again, Gregor was so infuriated that he turned in her direction as if to attack, but slowly and feebly. The cleaning woman, however, instead of being frightened, merely lifted high in the air a chair that was near the door, and, as she stood there with her mouth wide open, she clearly intended not to close her mouth again until the chair in her hand crashed down on Gregor's back. "So you're not advancing?" she asked as Gregor turned around again, and placed the chair back calmly in the corner.

By this time Gregor was hardly eating. Only when he accidentally passed by the spread-out food would he take a bit in his mouth playfully, hold it there for hours and then generally spit it out again. At first he thought it was his dejection over the state of his room that kept him from eating, but he was soon more reconciled to the changes in his room than to anything else. They had grown accustomed to put in his room things there was no space for elsewhere, and there were now a lot of such things, because they had rented one room in the apartment to three lodgers. These serious gentlemen — all three had full beards, as Gregor once ascertained through a crack in the door — were sticklers for strict housekeeping, not only in their room, but also, since

The Metamorphosis

1 **they** グレーゴルの家族　3 **foretokening** 〜の前触れの　4 **window panes** 窓ガラス　5 **her series of expressions** いつもの呼びかけ　6 **infuriated** かっとなった　7 **feebly** 弱々しく　8 **instead of being frightened** 怖がるどころか　12 **crashed down on Gregor's back** （椅子で）グレーゴルの背中を殴りつける　13 **advancing** やってくる、かかってくる

17 **spread-out food** （床に）ぶちまけてある食べ物　18 **playfully** 遊び半分に　**hold it there** 口の中に入れておいた　19 **spit it out** 吐きだした　20 **it was...that** (it was...that の強調構文) **dejection over** 〜に対する落胆、嫌悪　21 **reconciled** あきらめて受け入れた　22 **than to anything else** ほかのことと同様に　**They** 家族　23 **put in his room things** いろんな物を彼の部屋に入れる　**there was no space for elsewhere** ほかに（置く）余裕がない　25 **such things** そうやって彼の部屋に置かれた物　26 **lodgers** 間借り人　27 **ascertained** 確認した　28 **through a crack in the door** ドアのすき間から　**sticklers** 几帳面な人　**strict housekeeping** 家の中のことがきちんとなっていること

they were after all paying rent there, all over the apartment, and especially in the kitchen. They wouldn't stand for useless, not to mention dirty, odds and ends. Furthermore, they had for the most part brought along their own furnishings. Therefore many items had become superfluous that couldn't be sold but no one wanted to throw out. All of these were moved into Gregor's room. And so were the ash box and the garbage box from the kitchen. Whatever was unusable at the moment, the cleaning woman, who was always in a hurry, simply flung into Gregor's room; fortunately, Gregor generally saw only the object in question and the hand that held it. Perhaps the cleaning woman intended to retrieve the things when she had the time and opportunity, or to throw them all out at the same time, but in reality they remained wherever they had landed at the first toss, unless Gregor twisted through the rubbish and set it in motion, at first out of necessity, because no other space was open to crawl through, but later with increasing delight, although after such excursions, tired to death and dejected, he would again remain motionless for hours.

Since the lodgers sometimes also took their evening meal at home in the common parlor, the parlor door was closed on many evenings, but Gregor readily made do without the opening of the door, for on many earlier evenings when it was open he hadn't taken advantage of it, but instead, without the family noticing, had lain in the darkest corner of his room. But on one occasion the cleaning woman had left the door to the parlor a

1 **paying rent there** この家で家賃を払っているのだから　**all over the apartment**（not only...but also から続いている）この家全体に　2 **especially in the kitchen** とくにキッチンには　**stand for** 我慢する　3 **useless** 不要な　**not to mention dirty** 汚いのはいうまでもなく　**odds and ends** がらくた　4 **for the most part** ほとんど　5 **furnishings** 家財　**items** 家具など　6 **superfluous** 余分　7 **throw out** 捨てる　11 **flung into** 放りこんだ　12 **the object in question** 問題になっている物　**the hand that held it** それを持っている（家政婦の）手　13 **retrieve** 回収する　16 **wherever they had landed** それらが置かれた場所に　**at the first toss** 最初に放りこまれた　17 **twisted through the rubbish** 体をよじって、がらくたの間を抜ける　**set it in motion** がらくたを動かす　18 **out of necessity** 必要にかられて　19 **with increasing delight** 少しずつ喜びを感じるようになって　20 **excursions** 散歩　**tired to death and dejected** ぐったり疲れて、落ちこんでしまい

24 **made do** 対応した、適応した　26 **hadn't taken advantage of it** それを（ドアが開いていることを）利用する、活用することはなかった　27 **instead** そうはしないで、そうするどころか　**without the family noticing** 家族は気づかないまま　28 **on one occasion** あるとき

little open; and it remained open like that even when the lodgers entered in the evening and the light was turned on. They sat at the head of the table, where in earlier days the father, the mother and Gregor had sat; they unfolded their napkins and picked up their knives and forks. Immediately the mother appeared in the doorway with a platter of meat, and right behind her the sister with a plate piled high with potatoes. The food was steaming copiously. The lodgers bent over the plates that were placed in front of them as if wishing to examine them before eating, and, in fact, the one sitting in the middle, whom the others seemed to look up to as an authority, cut a piece of meat on the plate, obviously to ascertain whether it was tender enough and didn't perhaps need to be sent back to the kitchen. He was satisfied, and the mother and sister, who had watched in suspense, breathed easily and began to smile.

The family themselves ate in the kitchen. Nevertheless, before the father went into the kitchen, he entered the parlor and, with a single protracted bow, walked around the table, cap in hand. The lodgers all stood up and murmured something into their beards. Then, when they were alone, they ate with almost no conversation. It seemed odd to Gregor that, among all the multifarious noises of eating, their chewing teeth stood out again and again, as if to indicate to Gregor that teeth were indispensable for eating and that even with the finest toothless jaws nothing could be accomplished. "I do have an appetite," said Gregor uneasily to himself, "but not for

3 **at the head of the table** テーブルの上座（主人や客がすわる位置） **in earlier days** 以前は 7 **platter of meat** 肉をのせた大皿 **right behind her** 母親のすぐ後ろに 9 **steaming copiously** もうもうと湯気が立っている 10 **examine** 観察する 11 **the one sitting in the middle** まん中にすわっている間借り人 12 **look up to** 尊敬する **as an authority** 権威者として 14 **tender** 柔らかい 16 **in suspense** 緊張して、不安そうに

20 **protracted bow** ゆっくりとしたおじぎ 22 **murmured something into their beards** あごひげの中でぼそぼそいった 23 **they were alone** 3人きりになる 24 **the multifarious noises** 様々な音 25 **stood out** 目立った 26 **indispensable** 必要不可欠 27 **with the finest toothless jaws** どんなに立派なあごでも歯がなければ 28 **nothing could be accomplished** 何もできない（何も食べられない） 29 **uneasily** 不安そうに **but not for those things** あんなものには食欲はわかない

those things. How these lodgers pack it away, and I'm perishing!"

On that very evening — Gregor had no recollection of having heard the violin during that whole time — it was audible from the kitchen. The lodgers had already finished their supper, the one in the middle had pulled out a newspaper, handing one sheet apiece to the two others, and now they were leaning back, reading and smoking. When the violin began to play, they noticed it, stood up and walked on tiptoe to the hallway door, remaining there in a tight group. They must have been heard in the kitchen, because the father called: "Does the playing perhaps bother you? We can stop it at once." "On the contrary," said the gentleman in the middle, "wouldn't the young lady like to come in here with us and play in this room, which is much more comfortable and cozy?" "Of course," called the father, as if *he* were the violinist. The gentlemen stepped back into the room and waited. Soon the father came with the music stand, the mother with the sheet music and the sister with the violin. The sister calmly put everything in readiness for playing; the parents, who had never rented out rooms before and therefore overdid the courtesy due to lodgers, didn't dare to sit on their own chairs; the father leaned on the door, his right hand placed between two buttons of his closed uniform jacket; but the mother was offered a chair by one of the gentlemen and, since she left the chair where the man happened to have placed it, she sat off to one side in a corner.

1 **pack it away** 胃袋におさめる、平らげる **I'm perishing!** ぼくは死にかけている！
3 **recollection** 記憶 4 **during that whole time** このところずっと 5 **audible** きこえる 7 **one sheet apiece** 一枚ずつ 8 **leaning back** 椅子に背をあずけて 11 **in a tight group** ひとつ所に固まって **They must have been heard in the kitchen** 3人の足音がキッチンにまできこえたにちがいない 14 **On the contrary** 逆です、それどころか 17 **cozy** 居心地がいい、くつろげる 19 **the music stand** 譜面立て 20 **the sheet music** 楽譜 23 **overdid the courtesy due to lodgers** 間借り人に気を使いすぎた 27 **left the chair** 椅子を置いたままにした 28 **where the man happened to have placed it** その男がたまたま置いた場所に **sat off to one side** ぽつんと脇にすわった

The sister began to play; the father and mother, each on his side, watched the motions of her hands closely. Gregor, attracted by the playing, had ventured out a little further and already had his head in the parlor. He was scarcely surprised that recently he was so little concerned about the feelings of the others; previously this considerateness had been his pride. As it was, right now he might have had even more cause to hide, because as a result of the dust that had settled all over in his room and blew around at the slightest movement, he was also completely covered with dust; he was dragging threads, hairs and crumbs of food around with him on his back and sides; his indifference to everything was much too great for him to turn over on his back and scour himself on the carpet, as he used to do several times a day. But despite being in this state, he had no qualms about moving a little bit forward on the immaculate floor of the parlor.

To be sure, no one was paying attention to him. The family was completely engrossed in the violin performance; on the other hand, the lodgers, who, hands in trousers pockets, had first of all moved their chairs much too close behind the sister's music stand, so that they could all have looked at the sheet music, which assuredly had to disturb the sister, soon withdrew, with semiaudible remarks and lowered heads, to the window, where they stayed put, watched by the father with concern. It was now abundantly evident that they were disappointed in their assumption that they were going

1 **each on his side**（おそらく each on one's side のまちがい）それぞれの場所で　3 **ventured out** 思い切って出ていった　5 **was scarcely surprised** ほとんど驚かなかった　6 **this considerateness** このような気づかい　7 **As it was** 実際は　9 **had settled all over in his room** 彼の部屋中に積もっている　10 **blew around** あたり中に舞う　**at the slightest movement** ほんのかすかな動きでも　12 **crumbs of food** 食べかす　**his back and sides** 背中やわき腹　14 **turn over on his back** あお向けになる　**scour himself on the carpet** 絨毯に背中をこすりつける　16 **despite being in this state** こんな状態（様子）だったにもかかわらず　**qualms** 懸念、不安　17 **immaculate** 汚れやゴミがまったくない

20 **engrossed** 夢中になっている　22 **first of all** まず、まっ先に　24 **which** 間借り人たちが楽譜をみていること　25 **assuredly** まちがいなく　**withdrew...to the window**（間借り人たちは）窓まで下がった　26 **semiaudible remarks** 小声のつぶやき　27 **stayed put** 動かずにいる　28 **concern** 懸念、心配　**abundantly** 十分に　29 **assumption**（that 以下の）予想、思いこみ

to hear some pretty or entertaining violin music; they were clearly tired of the whole performance and were permitting their peace and quiet to be disturbed merely out of courtesy. It was especially the way they all blew their cigar smoke up into the air through their noses and mouths that indicated a terrific strain on their nerves. And yet the sister was playing beautifully. Her face was inclined to one side, her eyes followed the lines of music searchingly and sorrowfully. Gregor crawled a little bit further forward, keeping his head close to the floor in hopes of making eye contact with her. Was he an animal if music stirred him that way? He felt as if he were being shown the way to the unknown nourishment he longed for. He was resolved to push his way right up to his sister and tug at her skirt, as an indication to her to come into his room with her violin, because nobody here was repaying her for her playing the way he would repay her. He intended never to let her out of his room again, at least not as long as he lived; his horrifying shape was to be beneficial to him for the first time; he would be on guard at all the doors to his room at once, and spit at his assailants like a cat; but his sister would remain with him not under compulsion but voluntarily; she was to sit next to him on the couch and incline her ear toward him, and he would then confide to her that he had had the firm intention of sending her to the conservatory, and that, if the misfortune hadn't intervened, he would have told everyone so last Christmas — Christmas *was* over by now, wasn't it? — without listening to

3 **their peace and quiet** 静けさ、のんびりした時間　**merely out of courtesy** たんなる礼儀正しさから　4 **It was...that**（It was...thatの強調構文）　**the way**（あとに関係代名詞のthatを補って考える）様子　6 **a terrific strain** 大きな負担、緊張　7 **And yet** しかし　8 **the lines of music** 五線譜　12 **stirred him that way** こんなふうに彼を感動させた　13 **the unknown nourishment** それまで知らなかった栄養　14 **longed for** 切望していた　15 **tug at her skirt** 妹のスカートを引っぱる　**an indication** 指示　17 **repaying** 報いている　19 **at least** 少なくとも　**not** 部屋から出さない　20 **beneficial** 役に立つ　21 **on guard** 守る　22 **spit at his assailants like a cat** 攻撃者に向かって、猫みたいにフーッとうなる　23 **compulsion** 強制　**voluntarily** 自ら進んで　25 **confide** 打ち明ける　27 **the misfortune** こんな不幸　28 **would have told everyone so** みんなにそう話していただろう　29 **without listening to any objections** 反対意見には耳を貸さずに

any objections. After this declaration his sister would burst into tears of deep emotion, and Gregor would raise himself to the level of her shoulder and kiss her neck, which, since she had begun her job, she had left bare, without any ribbon or collar.

"Mr. Samsa!" the gentleman in the middle called to the father and, without wasting another word, pointed with his index finger to Gregor, who was moving slowly forward. The violin fell silent, the gentleman in the middle first smiled at his friends, shaking his head, and then looked at Gregor again. The father seemed to think that, to begin with, it was more necessary to placate the lodgers than to chase away Gregor, even though the men were not at all excited and Gregor seemed to entertain them more than the violin playing. He ran over to them and, with arms outspread, he tried to make them withdraw into their room, at the same time blocking their view of Gregor with his body. Now they actually got a little sore; it was no longer possible to tell whether this was due to the father's behavior or to the realization now dawning on them that, without their knowledge, they had had a next-door neighbor like Gregor. They demanded explanations from the father, they themselves now raised their arms, they plucked uneasily at their beards, and only slowly retreated toward their room. Meanwhile the sister had gotten over the state of total absence that had come over her after the abruptly terminated performance; after she had held the violin and the bow for some time in her limply hanging

2 **tears of deep emotion** 深い感動の涙　**raise himself** 体を起こす　4 **had left bare, without any ribbon or collar** リボンや襟をつけなくなったので、むきだしになっている
6 **"Mr. Samsa!"**（父親に対する呼びかけ）　7 **without wasting another word** それきり何もいわず　8 **index finger** 人差し指　12 **to begin with** まず最初に　13 **placate** なだめる　15 **entertain** 楽しませる　16 **with arms outspread** 両腕を広げて　18 **blocking their view of Gregor with his body** 自分の体で、間借り人たちがグレーゴルの姿をみないようにする　19 **got a little sore** ちょっと気分を害した、むっとした　21 **the realization now dawning on them that** (that 以下を) 彼らがいまわかりはじめたこと、理解しはじめたこと　**without their knowledge** 自分たちが知らないまま、自分たちに知らされないまま　24 **plucked** つまんだ　26 **had gotten over the state of total absence** まったくの放心状態から立ち直った　28 **abruptly terminated performance** 突然に終わった演奏　29 **the bow** バイオリンの弓　**limply** 力が抜けた状態、だらんと

hands and had continued to look at the music as if she were still playing, she had roused herself all at once; she had placed the instrument on the lap of her mother, who was still sitting on her chair gasping for breath, her lungs pumping violently, and had run into the adjoining room, which the lodgers were approaching more quickly now under pressure from the father. One could see the blankets and pillows on the beds fly up and arrange themselves neatly in the sister's skilled hands. Even before the gentlemen had reached their room, she had finished making the beds and slipped out. The father seemed once more so infected by his obstinacy that he forgot all the respect he after all owed his lodgers. All he did was crowd them and crowd them until, already in the doorway to the room, the gentleman in the middle stamped his foot resoundingly, thereby bringing the father to a halt. "I hereby announce," he said, raising his hand and looking around for the mother and sister as well, "that in view of the disgusting conditions prevailing in this apartment and family" — here he spat promptly on the floor — "I am giving up my room as of tomorrow morning. Naturally I won't pay a thing for the days that I've lived here, either; on the contrary, I'm going to think seriously about whether I shouldn't sue you — believe me, the proof wouldn't be hard to come by." He fell silent and looked straight ahead of him, as if he were expecting something. And, indeed, his two friends immediately chimed in with the words: "We're also leaving tomorrow." Thereupon he seized the door

1 the music 楽譜 2 roused herself 立ち上がる 4 gasping for breath あえいでいる 5 pumping 激しく動いている 7 under pressure from the father 父親の迫力に押されて 8 fly up 舞いあがる arrange themselves neatly きちんとなる（しわがのびる） 11 slipped out 抜けだした 12 infected 影響された obstinacy 頑固さ 13 after all あれほど owed 払っていた 14 crowd 押しやる 16 stamped his foot 足を踏み鳴らす resoundingly 大きな音を響かせて thereby それによって bringing the father to a halt 父親を立ち止まらせる 17 hereby ここに 19 in view of (of 以下のことを) 考えるに 20 prevailing はびこっている spat 唾を吐いた 21 promptly 素早く as of ～から 22 pay a thing まったく払わない 24 sue 訴える 25 believe me いいですか the proof 証拠、立証 come by 手に入れる、用意する 26 looked straight ahead of him まっすぐに目の前をみた 28 chimed in 同意した 29 Thereupon それをきっかけに、それを合図に

handle and slammed the door violently.

The father staggered to his chair with groping hands and let himself fall onto it; it looked as if he were stretching out for his customary evening nap, but the rapid nodding of his seemingly uncontrollable head showed that he was by no means asleep. Gregor had lain still the whole time on the same spot where the lodgers had detected him. The disappointment over the failure of his plan, but perhaps also the weakness caused by so much fasting, made it impossible for him to move. He was afraid that, almost as a certainty, everything would come tumbling down upon him at the very next moment; and he was waiting. Not even the violin startled him when it slipped from the mother's trembling fingers, fell off her lap and emitted a resounding note.

"Dear parents," the sister said, striking the table with her hand by way of preamble, "we can't go on like this. If you perhaps don't realize it, I do. In front of this monstrous creature I refuse to pronounce my brother's name, and therefore I merely say: we have to try to get rid of it. We've tried all that's humanly possible to take care of it and put up with it; I think no one can reproach us in the slightest."

"She's perfectly right," said the father to himself. The mother, who was still too short of breath, began to cough hollowly into the hand she held before her, with a crazed look in her eyes.

The sister ran over to the mother and held her forehead. The sister's words seemed to have helped the fa-

2 **staggered** よろよろ歩いた **with groping hands** 手探りをするような格好で 4 **stretching out** のびをしている **the rapid nodding** しきりにうなずくような動作 5 **his seemingly uncontrollable head** 思い通りにならないようにみえる頭 6 **by no means** 絶対に〜ではない 8 **detected** みつけた 9 **caused by** 〜に起因する、〜による 10 **fasting** 断食、食べないでいること 11 **as a certainty** 確実なこととして 12 **tumbling down upon him** 彼の上に崩れ落ちてくる 13 **startled** びっくりさせる 15 **emitted** 発した **a resounding note** 反響するような音 17 **by way of preamble** 話の前触れとして、話を始める合図として 19 **monstrous creature** 化け物、怪物 **pronounce my brother's name** 兄の名前を口にする 20 **get rid of** 排除する、ここから出ていかせる、なんとかする 21 **all that's humanly possible** 人としてできることすべて 22 **put up with** 耐えてきた 23 **in the slightest** 少しでも

25 **short of breath** 息が切れている 26 **hollowly** 弱々しく 27 **crazed look** 正気をなくしたような表情

28 **held her forehead** 母親の額に手を当てた

ther collect his thoughts; he had sat up straight and was playing with his messenger's cap between the dishes that were still left on the table after the lodgers' supper; and from time to time he looked over at the motionless Gregor.

"We have to try to get rid of it," the sister now said to her father only, because the mother, with her coughing, couldn't hear anything; "eventually it'll kill both of you, I can see it coming. When people already have to work as hard as all of us, they can't stand this perpetual torment at home, as well. I can't any more." And she burst into such a violent fit of weeping that her tears rained down onto her mother's face, from which she wiped them away with mechanical movements of the hand.

"My child," said the father sympathetically and with noticeable comprehension, "what are we supposed to do?"

The sister merely shrugged her shoulders to indicate the perplexity that had now taken hold of her during her crying fit, in contrast to her earlier self-confidence.

"If he understood us," said the father half-questioningly; in the midst of her tears she shook her hand violently to indicate that that was out of the question.

"If he understood us," repeated the father and, closing his eyes, absorbed in his own mind the sister's conviction of that impossibility, "then perhaps we could reach an agreement with him. But, as it is —"

"It's got to go," called the sister, "that's the only remedy, Father. All you have to do is try to shake off

1 **collect his thoughts** 考えをまとめる   **sat up straight** 背筋を伸ばした   2 **playing with** もてあそぶ   4 **looked over** みやる   8 **eventually** (このままだと) 最後は   10 **stand** 耐える   **this perpetual torment** 絶え間ない苦悩   11 **I can't** (stand)   12 **violent fit** 激しい発作   13 **from which** (which は her mother's face) **wiped them away** 涙をぬぐった   14 **mechanical movements** 機械的な動きで

15 **sympathetically** 共感して、同情して   16 **noticeable comprehension** よくわかったといわんばかりに   **what are we supposed to do?** われわれはどうすればいい？

18 **indicate** 示す   19 **perplexity** 当惑   **taken hold of** 支配した   21 **half-questioningly** 半ばたずねるかのように   22 **shook her hand** 手を振った   23 **out of the question** 問題外

25 **absorbed** 受け入れた   **conviction of that impossibility** (そんなことは) ありえないという確信   26 **then** そうであれば (グレーゴルがわれわれのいうことを理解できるのであれば) **reach an agreement with him** 彼と折り合いをつける

28 **It's got to go** あれには出ていってもらわないと   29 **remedy** 解決策   **shake off** 振り捨てる

the idea that that's Gregor. Our real misfortune comes from having believed it for so long. But how can it be Gregor? If it were Gregor, he would long since have realized that it's impossible for people to live side by side with an animal like that, and would have gone away of his own free will. Then we would have had no more brother, but we could go on living and honor his memory. But, as it is, this animal persecutes us, drives away our lodgers, and obviously wants to take over the whole apartment and make us sleep in the street. Just look, Father," she suddenly yelled, "he's starting again!" And, in a panic that Gregor couldn't understand at all, the sister even deserted her mother, literally hurling herself from her chair, as if she would rather sacrifice her mother than remain in Gregor's vicinity; she dashed behind her father, who, agitated solely by her behavior, also stood up and, as if protecting the sister, half-raised his arms in front of her.

But Gregor hadn't the slightest wish to frighten anyone, least of all his sister. He had merely started to turn around, in order to regain his room, and that was naturally conspicuous because in his ailing condition he could only execute those difficult turns with the aid of his head, raising it and bumping it on the floor many times. He stopped and looked around. His good intentions seemed to have been recognized; the panic had lasted only for a moment. Now they all looked at him in silent sorrow. The mother was slumped in her chair, her legs outstretched and pressed together; her eyes were

₂ **how can it be Gregor?** あれが兄さん（グレーゴル）であるはずがない　₃ **long since** ずっとまえに　₄ **side by side** いっしょに　₅ **of his own free will** 自らの意志で　₆ **Then** そうなったら（グレーゴルが出ていったら）　₇ **honor his memory** 兄さんの思い出を大切にする　₈ **as it is** 実際は（そうではなく）　**persecutes** 悩ます　**drives away** 追い出す　₁₃ **deserted** 見捨てた、母親を置いて逃げた　**hurling herself** 飛びだして　₁₄ **sacrifice** 犠牲にする　₁₅ **vicinity** 近く　₁₆ **agitated** 動揺した　**solely by her behavior** 妹の行動だけによって　₁₇ **half-raised his arms** 両腕を上げかけた

₂₀ **least of all his sister** 妹をおびえさせる気など、さらにない　₂₂ **conspicuous** 目立つ、目を引く　**ailing condition** 病的な状態　₂₃ **execute** 行う　**with the aid of his head** 自分の頭部を使って　₂₄ **bumping** ぶつけて　₂₈ **slumped** ぐったりしている　₂₉ **outstretched** 長く伸ばしていた　**pressed together** ぴったりくっつけていた

almost closing with exhaustion; the father and sister were sitting side by side; the sister had placed her hand around the father's neck.

"Now perhaps I can turn around," thought Gregor, and resumed his labors. He was unable to suppress the heavy breathing caused by the exertion, and had to stop to rest from time to time. Otherwise, no one was rushing him, everything was left to him. When he had completed the turn, he immediately began to head back in a straight line. He was amazed at the great distance that separated him from his room, and couldn't comprehend how, feeling so weak, he had just a while before covered the same ground almost without noticing it. His mind being constantly bent on nothing but fast crawling, he scarcely paid attention to the fact that he was not being disturbed by any word or outcry from his family. Only when already in the doorway did he turn his head, not all the way, because he felt his neck growing stiff, but enough to see that nothing had changed behind him except that his sister had stood up. His last look was at his mother, who had fallen asleep completely.

Scarcely was he inside his room when the door was hastily closed, barred and locked. The sudden noise behind him scared Gregor so badly that his little legs buckled. It was his sister who had been in such a rush. She had already been standing there on her feet and waiting, then she had leaped forward with light steps — Gregor hadn't heard her approaching — and she called "At last!" to her parents as she turned the key in the

The Metamorphosis

1 **with exhaustion** ぐったり疲れて
5 **resumed his labors** 苦行（方向転換）を続けた **suppress** 抑える 6 **exertion** 奮闘、大変な作業 7 **Otherwise** ほかの点では 9 **head back** もどる 10 **in a straight line** まっすぐに 13 **covered the same ground** 同じ距離を進んできた **without noticing it**（it は the great distance）気づきもしないで 14 **bent on** ひたすら心がけていた 16 **outcry** 叫び声 18 **not all the way**（首の曲げ方が）完全ではなかった **growing stiff** 凝ってきた

22 **Scarcely was he inside his room** 部屋に入るか入らないかのときに 23 **barred** かんぬきがかけられた 25 **buckled** がくっとなった **in such a rush** 大あわて 26 **on her feet** 立っていた 29 **At last!** ついにやった！　ああ、よかった！

lock.

"And now?" Gregor asked himself, and looked around in the darkness. He soon made the discovery that he could no longer move at all. This didn't surprise him; in fact, he found it unnatural that up until then he had actually been able to get around on those thin little legs. Besides, he felt relatively comfortable. True, he had pains all over his body, but he felt as if they were getting gradually milder and milder and would finally pass away altogether. By now he hardly felt the rotten apple in his back and the inflamed area around it, which were completely covered with soft dust. He recalled his family with affection and love. His opinion about the necessity for him to disappear was, if possible, even firmer than his sister's. He remained in this state of vacant and peaceful contemplation until the tower clock struck the third morning hour. He was still alive when the world started to become brighter outside the window. Then his head involuntarily sank down altogether, and his last breath issued faintly from his nostrils.

When the cleaning woman arrived early in the morning — in her natural strength and haste, despite frequent requests not to do so, she slammed all the doors so loud that throughout the apartment, from the moment she came, it was impossible to sleep peacefully — she found nothing out of the ordinary at first during her customary brief visit to Gregor. She thought he was lying motionless like that on purpose, acting insulted; she gave him credit for full reasoning powers. Because by

₂ **And now?** これからどうしよう？　₄ **he could no longer move at all** もう、まったく動けない　₅ **up until then** そのときまで　₈ **as if they** (they は pains)　₉ **pass away altogether** なくなってしまう　₁₁ **inflamed area** 炎症を起こしている部分　₁₄ **firmer** 〜以上に確固としたもの　₁₅ **this state of vacant and peaceful contemplation** ぼんやりと、おだやかに考えているこの状態　₁₈ **his head involuntarily sank down** 頭ががっくりたれた　₂₀ **nostrils** 鼻の穴

₂₂ **in her natural strength and haste** いつものように元気に、大急ぎで　**despite frequent requests not to do so** しないようにと何度もいわれているにもかかわらず（do so はこのあとの slammed all the doors so loud）　₂₆ **out of the ordinary** いつもと違っている　₂₇ **customary brief visit** お決まりの短時間の訪問　₂₈ **like that on purpose** わざとそうしているんだろうと　**acting insulted** ばかにされたと憤慨しているところをみせようと　₂₉ **gave him credit for** グレーゴルが（for 以下のものを）持っていると信じていた　**full reasoning powers** 十分な理性　**by chance** たまたま

chance she was carrying the long broom, she tried to tickle Gregor with it from her position in the doorway. When this proved fruitless, she became annoyed and jabbed Gregor a little, and only when she had moved him from the spot, without any resistance on his part, did she take notice. When she soon recognized the true state of affairs, she opened her eyes wide and gave a whistle, but didn't stay there long; instead, she tore open the bedroom door and shouted into the darkness: "Come take a look, it's croaked; it's lying there, a total goner."

The Samsas sat up in bed and were hard put to overcome the fright that the cleaning woman had given them until they finally grasped her announcement. Then Mr. and Mrs. Samsa got out of bed quickly, each on his side; Mr. Samsa threw the blanket over his shoulders, Mrs. Samsa came out wearing only her nightgown; in this way they entered Gregor's room. Meanwhile the parlor door had also opened; Grete had been sleeping there since the lodgers moved in; she was fully dressed as if she hadn't slept at all; the pallor of her face seemed to indicate that, too. "Dead?" asked Mrs. Samsa, and looked up questioningly at the cleaning woman, even though she was able to examine everything herself and could recognize it even without any examination. "I'll say!" replied the cleaning woman, and, as a proof, pushed Gregor's corpse another long way to the side with her broom. Mrs. Samsa made a motion as if to restrain the broom, but didn't do so. "Well," said Mr. Samsa, "now we can thank God." He crossed himself,

1 broom ほうき　2 tickle つつく　3 this proved fruitless 効果がないとわかる　4 jabbed 突いた　5 without any resistance on his part グレーゴルのほうからの抵抗はなかった　6 the true state of affairs 事の真相　7 gave a whistle 口笛を吹いた　9 Come take a look きて、みて　10 it's croaked あれが死んでますよ　a total goner 完全な死体

11 The Samsas ザムザ夫妻　were hard put to... 〜するのに苦労する　overcome 克服する　13 grasped 把握する　14 each on his side（おそらく each on one's side のまちがい）　16 in this way こんなふうに　19 fully dressed ちゃんと服を着ていた　20 the pallor 青白さ　23 examine 確かめる、確認する　24 recognize it（it はグレーゴルが死んでいること）　25 I'll say! 間違いありません！　26 pushed Gregor's corpse another long way グレーゴルの死体をもう一度ぐーっと押した　28 restrain the broom ほうきをおさえる　29 He crossed himself 十字を切った

and the three women followed his example. Grete, who didn't take her eyes off the corpse, said: "Just look how thin he was. Yes, he hadn't been eating anything for so long. The food came out of his room just the way it went in." Indeed, Gregor's body was completely flat and dry; actually that could be seen only now, when he was no longer lifted up on his little legs and nothing else diverted their attention.

"Come into our room for a while, Grete," said Mrs. Samsa with a melancholy smile, and, not without looking back at the corpse, Grete followed her parents into their bedroom. The cleaning woman shut the door and opened the window all the way. Despite the early morning hour, the fresh air already had a warm feeling to it. For by now it was the end of March.

The three lodgers stepped out of their room and, in amazement, looked around for their breakfast; the family had forgotten it. "Where's breakfast?!" the gentleman in the middle grumpily asked the cleaning woman. But she put her finger to her lips and then hastily and silently beckoned to the gentlemen to come into Gregor's room. They did so, and then, with their hands in the pockets of their somewhat shabby jackets, they stood around Gregor's corpse in the now completely bright room.

Then the bedroom door opened, and Mr. Samsa appeared in his uniform, with his wife on one arm and his daughter on the other. All of them had obviously been weeping; from time to time Grete pressed her face against her father's arm.

1 **followed his example** 父親と同じようにした 2 **take her eyes off the corpse** 死体から目を離す 4 **just the way it went in** 入ったときとまったく同じように 7 **nothing else diverted their attention** ほかには何も彼らの注意をそらすものがなかった

13 **opened the window all the way** 窓を大きく開けた 15 **For** というのも

19 **grumpily** 不満そうに 21 **beckoned** 合図した 23 **somewhat shabby jackets** なんとなくみすぼらしい上着

"Leave my home at once!" said Mr. Samsa, and pointed to the door, without freeing himself from the women. "What do you mean?" said the gentleman in the middle, somewhat taken aback, and put on a saccharine smile. The two others kept their hands behind their backs, rubbing them together uninterruptedly, as if in joyous anticipation of a major quarrel, which had to come out in their favor. "I mean exactly what I say," Mr. Samsa answered, and, with his two female companions, moved in a direct line toward the lodger. The latter stood still at first, looking at the floor, as if all the ideas in his head were being rearranged. "In that case, we're going," he then said, looking up at Mr. Samsa, as if, with a humility that was suddenly setting in, he were requesting new permission even for that decision. Mr. Samsa merely gave him a few brief nods, his eyes glaring. Thereupon the gentleman did indeed immediately take long strides into the hallway; his two friends, who for a while now had been listening with their hands completely at rest, now practically leaped after him, as if fearing that Mr. Samsa might enter the hall before them and cut off the liaison with their leader. In the hallway, all three took their hats off the hooks, drew their walking sticks out of the walking-stick stand, bowed in silence and left the apartment. With a mistrust that proved to be totally unjustified, Mr. Samsa and the two women stepped out onto the landing; leaning against the railing, they watched the three gentlemen descend the long staircase slowly but steadily, disappear on each floor into the

The Metamorphosis

2 **without freeing himself from the women** 女たちから離れないで 4 **taken aback** 身じろぎをして **a saccharine smile** 妙に甘い、へつらうような笑み 6 **uninterruptedly** しきりに、ずっと **joyous anticipation** うれしい期待 7 **a major quarrel** 大げんか **come out in their favor** 自分たちに都合のいい結果に終わる 8 **I mean exactly what I say** いっている通りの意味だ 10 **in a direct line** まっすぐに **The latter** 後者（the lodger） 12 **being rearranged** 整理されている **In that case** そういうことであれば 13 **humility** 謙虚さ 14 **setting in** 入りこむ 16 **glaring** にらみつけている **Thereupon** そこで 19 **with their hands completely at rest** 両手をまったく動かさないで 20 **leaped after him** 飛んで彼のあとを追った 21 **the liaison** つながり 24 **bowed in silence** 黙って頭を下げた 25 **a mistrust that proved to be totally unjustified** まったく根拠がないとわかった不信（間借り人たちが何かしでかすのではないかと思っていたが、そんな心配をする必要はなかった） 27 **the landing** 階段の上がり口 **leaning against the railing** 手すりにもたれて

same bend of the stairwell, and emerge again after a few moments; the lower they got, the more the Samsa family lost interest in them, and when a butcher boy, proudly bearing his tray on his head, met up with them and then climbed the stairs far above them, Mr. Samsa and the women left the railing, and they all returned to their apartment as if they were relieved.

They decided to spend that day resting and strolling; they not only deserved that pause from work, they absolutely needed it. And so they sat down at the table and wrote three letters of excuse, Mr. Samsa to the bank directors, Mrs. Samsa to the people who gave her piecework and Grete to her employer. While they were writing, the cleaning woman came in to say she was leaving because her morning chores were done. At first the three writers merely nodded, without looking up; it was only when the cleaning woman made no signs of going that they looked up in annoyance. "Well?" asked Mr. Samsa. The cleaning woman stood in the doorway smiling, as if she had a message that would make the family tremendously happy but would only deliver it if they questioned her thoroughly. The almost vertical little ostrich feather on her hat, which had annoyed Mr. Samsa all the time she'd been working for them, was waving slightly in all directions. "Well, what is it you want?" asked Mrs. Samsa, for whom the cleaning woman still had the most respect. "Yes," answered the cleaning woman, whose friendly laughter prevented her from continuing right away, "you don't have to worry your heads about

1 **bend of the stairwell** 階段の曲がっているところ 2 **the lower they got, the more the Samsa family lost interest in them** 彼らが下りていくにしたがって、ザムザ一家は彼らに興味をなくしていった 3 **a butcher boy** 肉屋の少年 7 **as if they were relieved** ほっとしたかのように

8 **strolling** 散歩 9 **deserved** 値した、相応しかった **pause** 休止 11 **excuse** 言い訳 12 **piecework** 職人仕事、肌着を縫う仕事 15 **chores** 仕事、用事 16 **it was only when...that** (it was...that の強調構文) 17 **no signs of going** いく様子がない 18 **in annoyance** どうしたのかと思って **Well?** どうした？ 20 **tremendously** とても 21 **deliver it** 伝える (it は a message) 22 **thoroughly** ちゃんと、しっかり **vertical** まっすぐ立っている **ostrich** ダチョウ 23 **annoyed** いらいらさせた 25 **in all directions** いろんな方向に 28 **whose friendly laughter** 親しげに声をあげて笑ったこと **continuing right away** すぐに言葉を続けること

how to clear out that trash next door. It's all taken care of." Mrs. Samsa and Grete lowered their heads to their letters, as if they wanted to go on writing; Mr. Samsa, who perceived that the cleaning woman now wanted to start describing everything in detail, forbade that decisively with an upheld hand. Now that she wasn't able to deliver a narration, she recalled the big hurry she was in; shouted, obviously peeved, "So long, one and all!"; turned on her heels furiously and left the apartment, slamming every door thunderously.

"We'll discharge her tonight," said Mr. Samsa, but received no reply from either his wife or his daughter, since the cleaning woman seemed to have once more disturbed the peace of mind they had just barely attained. They got up, went over to the window and stayed there, their arms around each other. Mr. Samsa turned around toward them on his chair and watched them silently for a while. Then he called: "Oh, come on over. Let bygones be bygones now. And have a little consideration for me, too." The women obeyed him at once, rushed over to him, caressed him and finished their letters quickly.

Then all three of them left the apartment together, something they hadn't done for months, and took the trolley out to the country on the edge of town. The car, in which they were the only passengers, was brightly lit by the warm sun. Leaning back comfortably on their seats, they discussed their prospects for the future, and it proved that, on closer examination, these were not at

1 trash ごみ　It's all taken care of 片づけました、処理しました　5 in detail 詳細に　forbade 止めた、やめさせた　6 with an upheld hand 片手を上げて　Now that ～になったので　7 deliver a narration 説明する（describing everything in detail）recalled the big hurry 大事な急用を思い出した　8 peeved 腹立たしげに　So long じゃあ、また　one and all みなさん　9 turned on her heels かかとでくるっと回った（背を向けた）
11 discharge 解雇する、くびにする　14 disturbed the peace of mind 心の平安を乱した　they had just barely attained ほんの少し前にやっと手に入れた　18 come on over こちらにおいで　19 Let bygones be bygones 過去のことは過去のことにしよう　20 consideration 思いやり　21 caressed him やさしくする、機嫌を取る
24 took the trolley 路面電車に乗った　25 the country 田舎　28 their prospects 予想、見込み　29 it proved that（that 以下のことが）わかった　on closer examination 細かく検討したところ

all bad, because the jobs that all three had, but which they hadn't really asked one another about before, were thoroughly advantageous and particularly promising for later on. Naturally the greatest immediate improvement in their situation would result easily from a change of apartment; now they would take a smaller and cheaper, but better located and in general more practical, apartment than their present one, which Gregor had found for them. While they were conversing in this way, Mr. and Mrs. Samsa, looking at their daughter, who was becoming more lively all the time, realized at almost the very same moment that recently, in spite of all the cares that had made her cheeks pale, she had blossomed out into a beautiful, well-built girl. Becoming more silent and almost unconsciously communicating with each other by looks, they thought it was now time to find a good husband for her. And they took it as a confirmation of their new dreams and good intentions when, at the end of their ride, their daughter stood up first and stretched her young body.

1 **which they hadn't really asked one another about** それまではおたがいにたずねたことがなかった 3 **advantageous** 見込みがある、有利な **particularly promising for later on** 今後の見通しが明るい、有望な 4 **the greatest immediate improvement** 大きな早急の改善 7 **better located** いい場所にある **in general** 全体として 9 **were conversing in this way** こんなことを話しながら 12 **cares** 心労や気苦労 14 **well-built** 体型の美しい 15 **unconsciously communicating** 無意識にコミュニケーションを取りながら 16 **by looks** 表情で 17 **took it as a confirmation** it（when 以下のこと）を（of 以下の）確証だと考えた 18 **good intentions** よかれと願うこと **at the end of their ride** 電車を降りるとき 19 **stretched her young body** 若い体でのびをした

あとがき

　フランツ・カフカ（1883年〜1924年）はプラハで生まれた。現在、プラハはチェコの首都だが、当時はボヘミア王国の首都だった。カフカは若い頃から文学好きだったが、父親の意見に従って、プラハ大学で法律を専攻し、卒業後、役所に勤務することになる。しかし一方で創作活動に励み、41歳で死ぬまでに数々のユニークな作品を残した。

　カフカはマックス・ブロートという友人に、自分が死んだら、原稿や手紙やメモなどすべてを焼き捨てるようにと遺言した。だが、ブロートはその遺言には従わず、カフカの残したものを編集し直して出版した。

　第2次世界大戦後、カフカは世界的に広く読まれるようになっていく。

　代表作は『変身』のほか、長編では『失踪者』『審判』『城』など。また短編小説の評価も高く、カフカの影響をうけた作家や文学者も多い。

　とまあ、どこの文学事典にでも載ってそうなことを簡単にまとめるとこんな感じだ。

　ところでこの『変身』だが、いろんな人がいろんなふうに語っているし、事実、いろんな読み方ができる。

　たとえば、いきなり一家の重荷になった人と家族との関係を寓話風に描いた作品という読み方もできる。そういうふうに読むと、この作品はずいぶん暗い。アメリカ20世紀を代表する作家カート・ヴォネガット

は『国のない男』のなかで次のように書いている。

　主人公の若者はかなり不細工で、人好きのするほうではない。親族との関係もあまりうまくいってなくて、仕事は忙しいが、昇進の見込みはない。女の子をダンスに連れていったり、仲間とビヤホールで一杯やる程度の給料ももらっていない。ある朝、目が覚めてみると、また仕事に行く時間で、気づくとゴキブリになっていた。とことん暗い話だ。

『変身』を読む限り、主人公がどんな虫になったのかははっきり書かれていないので、ヴォネガットみたいに「ゴキブリ」と決めつけてはいけないと思うし、グレーゴルも「ビヤホールで一杯やる程度の給料」はもらっているような気がする。しかし、こういう読み方をすると、たしかに暗い話だ。
　一方、カフカが仲間の前で『変身』を朗読したときのことも有名だ。まえがきで引用させてもらった新田さんの文章でも「カフカは、『変身』の最初の部分を友だちに語って聴かせたことがあります。みんな笑ったそうです」と書かれている。もちろんカフカがそういう読み方をしたのだろう。
　とすると、これは悲劇的な状況を悲劇的に捉えていない（捉えられない）男を、ユーモラスに、辛辣に描いた作品なのかもしれない。そもそもグレーゴルは朝起きて、虫になっているのに、それをあまり嘆いていないし、二度寝して起きてみたら6時半で、4時に目

あとがき

覚ましかけておいたのに、会社、どうしよう……などと悩んでいる。おいおい、という感じだ。
　そんなグレーゴルをみていると、これって、もしかしたら現代人そのものなのかもしれないという気もしてくる。
　その他にも様々な読み方のできる作品だと思う。
　ぜひ、じっくり読んでみてほしい。

　　　　　　　　　　　　　　　　　　　金原瑞人

[著者]
フランツ・カフカ　Franz Kafka

チェコ出身のドイツ語作家(1883-1924)。プラハのユダヤ人の家庭に生まれ、プラハ大学で法律を専攻、卒業後、役所に勤務するかたわら創作活動に励む。不安と孤独のただようユニークな作品を残した。第２次世界大戦後、カフカは世界的に広く読まれるようになり、影響を受けた文学者も多い。代表作は『変身』のほか『失踪者』『審判』『城』など。

[編者]
金原瑞人（かねはら・みずひと）

法政大学教授、翻訳家。ヤングアダルト小説をはじめ海外文学の紹介、翻訳で著名。著書『翻訳のさじかげん』(ポプラ社)ほか。訳書『豚の死なない日』(ロバート・ニュートン・ペック、白水社)『青空のむこう』(アレックス・シアラー、求龍堂)『国のない男』(カート・ヴォネガット、ＮＨＫ出版)ほか多数。編著『金原瑞人 MY FAVORITES　THE BOX』(ブルース・コウヴィル、青灯社)。

金原瑞人 MY FAVORITES
変身 THE METAMORPHOSIS

2012年7月30日　第1刷発行

著者　　フランツ・カフカ
編者　　金原瑞人
発行者　辻一三
発行所　株式会社青灯社
東京都新宿区新宿 1-4-13
郵便番号 160-0022
電話 03-5368-6923（編集）
　　 03-5368-6550（販売）
URL http://www.seitosha-p.co.jp
振替　00120-8-260856
印刷・製本　株式会社シナノ
© Mizuhito Kanehara 2012
Printed in Japan
ISBN978-4-86228-059-6 C0082

小社ロゴは、田中恭吉「ろうそく」（和歌山県立
近代美術館所蔵）をもとに、菊地信義氏が作成

●青灯社の英語の本

英単語イメージハンドブック
定価1800円＋税

大西泰斗（東洋学園大学教授）

1冊で基本的な英単語のイメージがすべて分かる集大成。

英語力が飛躍するレッスン
〜音読・暗写・多読のメソッド公開
定価1429円＋税

今井康人（立命館慶祥中学校・高等学校教諭）

音読を中心に、多数の高校生で実証された本物の英語上達法。

英語世界の表現スタイル 〜「捉え方」の視点から

吉村公宏（奈良教育大学教授）
定価1500円＋税

英語圏では言いたいことから一直線に表現する方法を好む。日本人はうず潮型の表現を好むから海外で理解されにくい。

語源で覚える英単語 3600
定価1700円＋税

藤井俊勝（東北福祉大学教授）

接頭辞19種と語根200種の組み合わせで覚える、効率的な単語増強法。

英語のかけ込み寺
〜TOEIC400点台から900点へ

I 単語をうまく使う
II 簡潔な文をつくる
III 国際英語の仲間入り

片野拓夫（英語のかけ込み寺主宰）
定価各2000円＋税

TOEIC800点台が続出。本気の英語学習者向け、カリスマ講師の全3冊決定版。

金原瑞人 MY FAVORITES
THE BOX
定価1200円＋税

ブルース・コウヴィル著　金原瑞人編

英語圏で大人気の児童文学作家のやさしい短編を、金原瑞人氏の詳しい注つきで辞書なしに読む。